The Ancient Maya

In Yucatán (Mexico) and Central America lives one of the most indestructible people in the world's history: the Maya. From earliest times to the present, they have kept their identity and their language through changes and disasters that would have crushed most peoples. This book gives an account of the Maya with emphasis on their great past civilization.

The Maya were great mathematicians and advanced artists. Their surviving books introduce us to a practical system of time measurement that calculated the movements of the visible planets and the length of the solar year with as great accuracy as our own. They built populous cities of stone, and lived a very full life without using either the wheel or metal. Why this great civilization should have broken down in the late tenth century AD remains one of the great mysteries of archaeology. Still the Maya people and much of their way of life survived, and today Maya remains a living language of great importance in Yucatán and Guatemala.

In this well-illustrated book the author gives a vivid and informative account of a civilization that flourished for over two thousand years, and that has given much to mankind, including rubber, cocoa, and vanilla.

By the same author:

THE AZTECS

FINDING OUT ABOUT THE INCAS

Other books for the Young Historian, uniform with this volume:

ANCIENT CHINA   *Cornelia Spencer*

ANCIENT CRETE   *Frances Wilkins*

ANCIENT EGYPT   *Roger Lancelyn Green*

ANCIENT JAPAN   *J. Edward Kidder*

ANCIENT RUSSIA   *Melvin C. Wren*

ANCIENT SCANDINAVIA   *George L. Proctor*

IMPERIAL ROME   *H. E. Mellersh*

REPUBLICAN ROME   *E. Royston Pike*

THE YOUNG HISTORIAN BOOKS *Edited by Cyril Green, MA*

The Ancient Maya

BY C. A. BURLAND

DRAWINGS BY ELIZABETH HAMMOND

THE JOHN DAY COMPANY

New York

In Memory of R. H. Dalgety

Acknowledgements

Photographs in this book are reproduced by kind permission of the Trustees of the British Museum.

Second Impression

Published by The John Day Company, Inc. 62 West 45th Street, New York, N.Y. 10036.

Library of Congress Catalog Card Number 67-10822
PRINTED IN THE UNITED STATES OF AMERICA

Contents

List of Illustrations

Aids to pronunciation of Maya words

Remember that the Maya learned to use the European alphabet from Spanish missionaries, so we really have to use a Spanish pronunciation of the letters. There are two rather special sounds; *PP* which is a violent *P* sound, and *Dz* which used to be written with a special symbol, a reversed *C*. One can approximate it by trying to pronounce *dz* at once as one letter.

The vowels are of the Latin type:

a = ah, as in Sh*ah*.

e = e, as in g*e*t when short; when long, it sounds rather like the exclamation "eh?"

i = i, as in vacc*i*ne; when short, it is like *i* in h*i*t.

o = o, as in h*o*t; when long, the same sound is drawled.

u = u, as in p*u*ssy; when long, it is like *oo* in r*oo*m.

Every letter is sounded. Thus Campeche is not sounded as Cam-peach, but as Cam-pe-che.

The diphthongs *ch* and *sh* are as in English; *th* is an aspirated *t*. Try to say it as *t* and breathe out at the same time. *Qu* is a *k* sound. *X* is now pronounced as *sh*.

One tries to accent the words as in Spanish – that is, on the antepenultimate syllable, as in MAY-a-pan, and YUC-a-tec. But shorter words are accented on the first of two syllables – BOL-on, QUI-che.

When there is an exception, one sees an acute accent mark, as in Itzá = It-ZA.

Do not be afraid of long words; just split them up into syllables, and take them slowly. Try *Chac-an-po-ton*, *Dzi-bal-an-che*, and so on. But so many Maya words are very simple in form, as single syllables, that it is not really difficult.

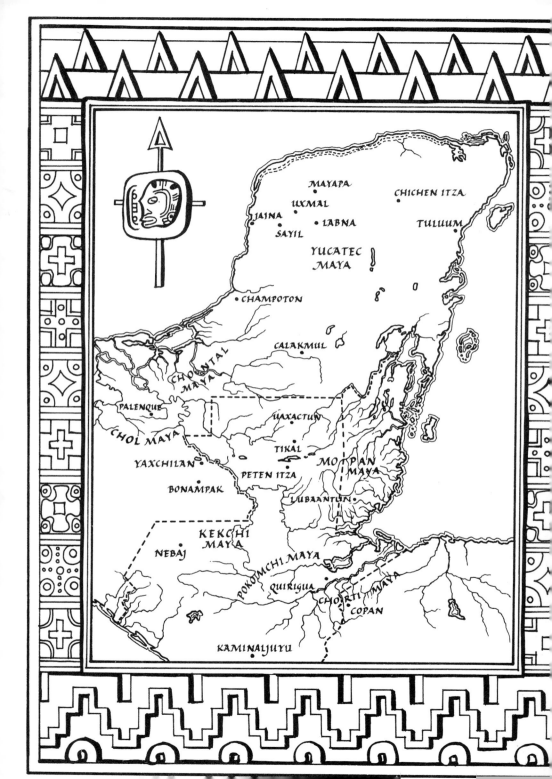

MAYAPA

UXMAL

CHICHEN ITZA

JAINA

LABNA

TULUUM

SAYIL

YUCATEC
MAYA

CHAMPOTON

CALAKMUL

CHONTAL
MAYA

PALENQUE

UAXACTUN

CHOL MAYA

TIKAL

YAXCHILAN

MO PAN
MAYA

PETEN ITZA

BONAMPAK

LUBAANTUN

KEKCHI
MAYA

NEBAJ

POKOMCHI MAYA

QUIRIGUA

CHORTI MAYA

COPAN

KAMINALJUYU

The Cities in the Forest

OVER the eastern slopes of the cordillera, passing through *The Maya lands*
Guatemala, Honduras, and San Salvador and over the
lowlands between the mountains (which extend into British
Honduras) and the dry limestone plateau of Yucatán, a
great rain forest covers the land. In this green land, trails
are few, and the jungle is so thick that even stone pyramids,
covered by trees and creepers, are invisible from thirty
or forty yards away.

Toward the end of the eighteenth century a book, *The* *First discovery*
Ruins of an Ancient City, appeared. It was written by Del
Rio and Cabrera, and describes how in southern Mexico,
ground was being cleared for a plantation, and suddenly
a group of buildings was exposed. The solid low buildings
had ornamental crests on the roof and were erected on
pyramids. Nobody had any clue to the history or origins of
the place. No name survived; the local Maya Indian
families had no tradition about it. The explorers named it
from the palisade which was being put up around the estate.
It became known as Palenque ("Palisade").

In the midnineteenth century an American consul, *First book about*
John Lloyd Stevens, traveled extensively in Guatemala and *the Maya*
Honduras. He took the artist Frederick Catherwood with
him to make a pictorial record of several remarkable monuments which were known to exist in the forest, often in
lonely places where there were few plantations and only
scattered settlements of the Lacandon Indians. Their
publications first revealed to the general public that this
region of Central America had been the home of a magnificent civilization. Catherwood's exquisite lithographs
gave accurate representations of the strange sculptures and 9

Map of the Maya lands in Mexico, Guatemala, Honduras and British Honduras,
showing principal towns

monuments of the Maya cities, especially of the great townsite of Copán in Honduras.

Chichén Itzá

At that time there was no way of linking the inscriptions or the buildings with any known civilization. But later on, the great city of Chichén Itzá ("At the Well Mouth of the Itzá") was studied. Its ruined pyramids were not far from Mérida, the capital of Yucatán, and everybody knew that at the time when the Spaniards conquered Mexico, this had been an important city of the Maya people. They did not realize just how great was the difference between Chichén Itzá and the Maya cities in the great forests, but they correctly identified the unknown cities as being the work of Maya Indians, from whom most of the present-day inhabitants of Yucatán are descended.

The puzzle of the dates

In the Archives of the Indies, in Spain, there was a book written by the first Bishop of Yucatán, Diego de Landa. After nearly three centuries of neglect it was found that this book contained an abbreviated account of Maya writing. Bishop Landa had questioned the wisest men he could find, and they told him that some of their hieroglyphs could be read as sounds like those of the Spanish alphabet. Scholars soon realized that the signs written down by Landa were like those they had seen copied from the ancient monuments in the forest. Because the Maya used syllables, but not a true alphabet, Landa's little collection of these signs was of small help. However, he gave an exact account of the symbols they used in counting time, and it became possible to decipher the dates and the astronomical facts recorded on Maya monuments. It became clear that these ancient cities contained inscriptions which had been made at various times over something like 1,000 years. By the end of the nineteenth century it was possible to arrange series of the monuments in order of date and to see how the style of art had changed in time. This was not a vague sequence dating, but very exact dating down to individual days, and entirely in Maya symbols. Nobody knew exactly where the Maya calendar could be fitted into the Christian calendar, and this problem of correlating the two systems

Design with Maya inscription, from the Temple of the Owls,
at Chichén Itzá. This records a transit of Venus in the twelfth
century

of dating has long been a source of confusion and debate.

With the discovery of dating by radioactive carbon 14,
it became possible to take pieces of wood from buildings
which showed Maya dates and to find their age within
half a century. At first the dates from different sites did
not agree, but further tests have brought an average correlation of dates within the system proposed by J. H. Good-

*The answer to the
puzzle*

11

man, Martínez-Hernández and J. Eric S. Thompson. The differences between the three were so small that astronomical data could be used for a final check, and a transit of Venus in the twelfth century recorded at Chichén Itzá placed the correlation with the Martínez variation. After the Maya had abandoned the ancient cities of the forest lands at the beginning of the tenth century, the calendar was kept less and less carefully, but a few records made after the Spanish conquest gave Maya dates in an abbreviated style, as well as Spanish dates; the best of them fit well with the accepted correlation. The linkages between them and the better understood system of dating used by the Aztecs have been made clear by J. Eric S. Thompson in his book *Maya Hieroglyphic Writing*.

Placing the Maya culture   It is now known that the greatest days of the Maya fell in the early centuries of the Christian era, principally in the period between Constantine and Charlemagne in European history or of the Han and T'ang dynasties in China. The finest cities and the most detailed inscriptions belong to the ancient sites discovered in the great forest. There the flowering of a civilization occurred. It was technically in the Stone Age, but its makers showed abilities which brought it level with other older civilizations of the Bronze Age in the Mediterranean. However, these all passed away 1,000 years before the Maya began their strange inscriptions in the distant land where no news of the civilizations of the Old World had ever penetrated.

The Maya Indians were among the world's pioneers on the path of civilization, and because of that, they are worthy of study, as well as because of their interesting and strange life and their own special ways in art. The following pages tell something of the story of these fascinating people, whose past has been discovered only in the last century.

CHAPTER ONE

The Maya People

THE Maya were a large group of American Indians living *The people*
in what is now southern Mexico, Guatemala, and parts of
San Salvador and Honduras. They spoke several related
languages, but with a range of variation as great as that
among the Romance languages of Europe. Physically the
Maya peoples were short and strongly built. They were
typical of the older groups of American Indians before
the tall people of the Plains tribes entered the continent.
They all had straight black hair, although a few individuals
developed a wavy structure in their long tresses. Their skin
colors varied over a wide range of rather coppery-brown
tints. They had large brown eyes with a typical Mongolian
fold on the inner sides of the eyelids. The women were
small, and few of them had well-marked waists.

We presume that many thousands of years ago the an- *The migration*
cestors of the American Indians had infiltrated the continent
by way of a dry land bridge across the area of the Bering
Strait. They had moved down very slowly from one place
to another, living by hunting. We do not know when the
Maya separated from other tribes or when they developed
their distinctive language. In all probability these were
events of the period when the tribes were discovering
agriculture in their new tropical homeland. The historic
Maya considered that they had always lived in the area
where they are settled today. The legends tell of ancestral
heroes emerging from corn plants, but there is no migration
legend.

The Maya had no great interest in history. There are
a series of prophetic books which record a sequence of
events linked to the calendrical system, but these Books of 13

Chilan Balam, as they are called, do not take us back beyond the period of the Toltec invasion of Yucatán in the latter part of the tenth century. One of the Books seemed to have earlier records, but it was worked over methodically by the late R. F. Dalgety, who proved it to be a triple repetition of the same events with slight variations in each version. At the present state of decipherment of Maya hieroglyphic writing it appears that nearly all the surviving material relates to the calendar and its linkages with mythology. There is little hope of recovering any detailed and connected series of historical records.

Maya monuments   We are left with almost entirely archaeological data, which are aided by comparisons of artistic styles from dated monuments. This is made clear for each of the Maya cities by groups of inscribed monuments, mostly free-standing blocks of stone which we describe as *stelae*. These stelae are usually carved with the figure of a deity presiding over the fortunes of the time period in which they were erected and with a date expressed with great accuracy, often with astronomical details added.

The monuments are not found lying around alone; they are normally assembled in groups and appear in association with "pyramids," which are really flat-topped structures supporting temples. The whole Maya area is scattered with such sites.

City ruins   The average Maya city center was built on a masonry platform. One approached through the outskirts of the town, sometimes along a raised causeway of white limestone. Such short roads, or *sacbeob*, were probably built more for processions than for transport. The path came to the raised platform, which one ascended by a wide range of short steps, which were some eight inches high but with a tread often as shallow as four inches. Then one was faced by a beautiful open plaza, always kept clean, for it was the pride of the local people. At the far end stood a huge pyramidal structure with a broad flat top. It rose in stages, and crossing them all vertically would be a broad steep staircase, running 14 in one sweep right to the top. At the top there would be a

The tallest known Maya stela, from Quiriguá. The feathered god probably
represents Kukulcan. The inscription on the side is concerned with astronomical
data including at the top a Long Count date. Early Maya Classic

stone house, with a towering high roof crest decorated with fantastic sculptures. On each side of the courtyard there were other pyramids and temples with god houses on top, and often at the entrance there would be ranges of longer, lower buildings, also on solid pyramidal mounds. These were the houses of chiefs and priests.

In the courtyard stood isolated carvings, sometimes in one row and sometimes grouped at the foot of the main temple. These monuments were not tablets of history, but magical stones which recorded the passing of time. On these were figures of gods and long inscriptions carved as beautifully as possible and made more clear by paints of many brilliant colors.

The ceremonial centers In the days of Maya glory these centers were meant for the service of the gods. There was always some activity, but on the festival days, one of which fell on every twentieth day of the calendar, there were brilliant ceremonies, in which public sacrifices were performed by the priests. However, none but qualified priests climbed the pyramid steps to the temples, and inside them only the greatest of priests dared venture before the images of the gods and the sacred writings which told of the mysteries of time and fate.

In the courtyard on great occasions there would be a multitude of men dressed in their most elaborate loincloths and headdresses, each according to his social rank. Women would not be allowed to come into this holy place, for they were regarded as having a great magic of their own. They took part in the festivals, but only in the outer courtyards, where their power did not clash with the other magic of warriors and chiefs. Apart from a very general plan, however, each Maya city center differed from every other. They all were individual constructions, made according to local styles.

Population The number and size of these buildings suggest that the population in ancient times was much larger than at present. It has been supposed that in ancient times the ceremonial centers with the temples and sacred courtyards were lonely

16

places inhabited by priests and visited by the people from the surrounding farmlands only on the festivals. But recent excavations at Tikal in Guatemala have shown that the ceremonial center there was surrounded by thousands of habitation mounds which once supported wooden houses. Among these are lesser centers of stone buildings and pyramids. It seems that Tikal in the fifth and sixth centuries AD, was an organized metropolis with a very large resident population, which presumably lived by intensive cultivation, not only of garden plots around the houses, but also cornfields some distance away.

The civilization which the Maya built for themselves was influenced by contact with other peoples, first by the so-called Olmecs, who built up a civilization with pyramidal temple mounds and magnificent stone sculptures as early as 900 BC. These Olmecs (so called because they lived in the land which later Mexicans called the Rubber or "Olli," district invented the art of writing in symbolic forms which look somewhat like the syllabary used by the Maya in later times. To the north of the Maya was the land of the Zapotecs, who built towns and left inscriptions as early as the third or fourth century BC. Contemporary with the early days of the Maya cities a great Mexican civilization was centered on the holy city of Teotihuacán, a little north of the present Mexico City. At one site in the highlands of Guatemala, known to us as Kaminaljuyú, the Teotihuacano people were so strongly represented that we think they had either a great trading center or, more likely, considering later Mexican history, a powerful military garrison, which dominated the local Maya people and protected the roads for merchants trading among the Maya lowland settlements.

Contact with other peoples

We can have no doubt that the Maya developed their civilization under the influence of the Olmecs, the Zapotecs, and the Teotihuacanos, too. Yet they developed their own ideas of temple building and writing to a very high degree. The writing itself differs from other systems used in Central America. Whatever the content of the other systems the number of glyphs known is fewer than that of the Maya,

17

who used nearly 700. Without any influence from the Old World the Maya developed a syllabic system of writing sounds which had truly phonetic values rather than direct pictorial meanings. Of all the ancient peoples of America, the Maya achieved the most advanced system of recording thought as expressed in words.

Maya arts   In painting, sculpture, and architecture, the Maya equaled the best of any other ancient American civilization and developed a style which is distinctively their own. It is well balanced, but florid in the extreme. Color was used not only in wall paintings, but also on every piece of sculpture. In the tropical light the Maya cities must have been a sight of fantastic splendor.

Textiles were woven in the most elaborate ceremonial designs, sometimes painted, sometimes embroidered with gaily colored thread. Feathers of tropical birds were obtainable in abundance, and garments covered in featherwork were worn by notable people. Headdresses of fantastic form were made of bark paper and plumage. Jewels of jade and shell were worn as ear ornaments, collars, wristlets, and anklets. Hard jade of many differing mineral compositions was cut, bored, carved and polished by the use of abrasive sand.

In pottery excellent forms were made and decorated by carving and painting. No wheel was used by potters, but their skill in forming the many types of vessel used in daily life, as well as in the temples, was truly remarkable. Pots were painted or carved; sometimes they were orange, sometimes black, but they were always of fine craftsmanship.

Yet this brilliant people lived in a Stone Age, having no use for metals and indeed no knowledge of them until late in their history, when the Toltecs from the Mexican highlands brought bronze bells and chisels. They had no gold in their country, but occasionally gold came to them by trade, mostly in the form of ready-made ornaments from the tribes of Panama.

Foodstuffs   Maya civilization depended largely on the cultivation
18   of corn. The wild animals, including deer, were insufficient

to provide much meat for such a large population, although some semiwild peccaries were kept available, and there were flocks of tame turkeys. Wild and cultivated fruits were enjoyed, but the real staple was corn. There was little attempt to elaborate on the ancient method of shifting cultivation every few years from one plot of ground to another, in order to let the soil recover its fertility.

Whether the excess of population, climatic change, or exhaustion of the soil was the cause, sometime just after AD 900 the ancient cities of the Maya in the mountains and forest were abandoned, and the cities in the dry limestone area of Yucatán became the heirs of the old Maya culture. For some time the Yucatec cities fell under the domination of Toltec warrior chiefs who had escaped from the civil wars which occasioned the fall of the Toltec empire in Mexico, but eventually the Maya regained full independence. When they were discovered by Europeans in the early sixteenth century, they were living in prosperous city-states, engaged in trade on a large scale, but chronically at war with one another. Their internal dissensions led to a rapid collapse, but in the centuries to the present time, the Maya have lost neither their identity nor their language.

The astonishing persistence of Maya culture always *Individual art* involved the love of local freedom, not so much for the *styles* individual as for the families of a district. In the ancient cities the styles of art vary from site to site, reflecting this strong spirit of local independence. All the cities used local stone for building, although some preferred to place solid masonry over a rubble core, others to use thinner facing stones, and others to set their stones in massive cement grouting. Still others seem to have remained content with clay. Surprisingly, some of them baked clay into brick and became the only people in ancient America to use this medium for building. At first sight all Maya sculptures may seem to be very much alike, but it is soon clear to the careful student that there are differences of style which can be used, not only to date the monument, but also to tell in which of the major cities it originated. For instance, the 19 strong static figures from Copán contrast widely with the flowing lines and elegant relief in stucco which characterize Palenque.

Maya wars The spirit of independence, shown by diversities in art and sometimes in religion, was reflected in political life, probably at all periods of Maya history. The Maya cities of Yucatán were involved in wars with one another at the time of the Spanish conquest, but that was not degeneracy. As early as the eighth century AD the wonderful frescoes at Bonampak depicted a fierce war and the mutilation of prisoners. At Tikal, remains were found of some ceremonial stelae which had been smashed down at some period in the past and then reerected. This looks like a recovery after some invasion in which the time markers of the city were destroyed. The violence of such an attack which broke up sacred objects need not surprise us. The Maya character is steady, serious, not easily provoked, but when tensions have risen high, the explosion has been violent. In any case there are plenty of records to show that in ancient Mexico it was a recognized practice, when a town was captured, to burn the temples and destroy the sacred books in an attempt to deprive the losers of their powers of magic.

The pattern of history Perhaps the best way to consider Maya history is to compare it with the pattern of politics in Renaissance Italy, where wonderful achievements in science and art ran evenly with a history of family feuds and intercity wars. The parallel is the closer when we consider that the mass of the people spoke the same national language, cultivated the same foodstuffs, dressed alike, and followed the same religious observances.

The concept of the unified state comprising all the people of the group and all their cities was apparently not of importance among the Maya. For a time in later history it was imposed by the invading Toltec lords of Chichén Itzá, but it did not last long. The Maya found freedom in their diversities, and very likely this attitude of mind increased their pride in local achievements in art and astronomical magic.

20

Above Limestone statue of the corn-god, showing the young plant sprouting from his head. From Copán. Maya Classic

Below Carving from Yaxchilán showing two noblemen, a warrior with his stone spear, and a priest dressed as the rain-god. Maya Classic

CHAPTER TWO

The Gods and the Calendar

Maya ceremonies AT the very beginnings of the story of the Maya, their artistic style is well developed and characteristic. It could be nothing but Maya. There is no other style with which it could be confused. Maya art has been employed in the service of religion from its beginning. When pottery is painted, all the designs can be interpreted as the symbols of the religious cults. Throughout history there has been no people, with the possible exception of the Tibetans, whose life has been so closely united with their religious beliefs.

One cannot explain the Maya civilization without trying to find how the Maya conceived of the universe and the mysterious powers which controlled fate. As we have noted, the Maya calendar was so arranged that a public festival fell once every twenty days. This religious festival was the occasion when people came to the great temples in the heart of the cities to witness the magical ceremonies and dances of the priests and to take part themselves. These were by no means all solemn occasions; there were plenty of opportunities for joyful celebrations, in which flowers were thrown and gifts exchanged. Some of them involved a great deal of heavy drinking of the intoxicating honey wine known as *balche*. The festival day was also a market day. The visitors to the town, as well as the citizens, would arrange barter deals and make the festival a great occasion for secular business. One may be sure that they felt it all was part of the one religious occasion. After all, many of the gods were depicted in their magic books as merchants carrying their burdens.

The great gods The chief of the gods was Hunabku, but most people

22 revered his son as Lord of Life. He was named Itzamna,

A post Classic Maya town and market, with the market chief on a throne and traders coming by canoe. In the distance a chief is carried in his hammock

and is usually shown as an old wrinkled man accompanied by an equally aged goddess. They were the creative powers of male and female, and were thought of as beings who existed before anything else. Below the creator came many layers of the heavens, which were the places where the stars moved and the planets flew among them. There were also heavens of light and of the sun and moon. The shooting stars had their sphere, and there was a heaven of the clouds and rainbows. At the four corners of the earth were holy places where gods lived like giants holding up the sky. Then there were spirits of all living things. The gods were represented in all kinds of activities and protected their followers in various trades, where they were respected in much the way that members of medieval European trade guilds respected their patron saints. Below the level of the earth were the series of nine underworlds, where traps were set so that when the dead finally arrived in the underworld, which was called Xibalba, they were simply skeletons.

The way of the sun   All the gods had differing forms, mostly according to the magic of the four directions, which changed the nature of everything because they were the different magics of the sun. Ah Kin was the sun-god, Lord of Day. He rose in the east and so brought blessings to growing things; he reached his height in the south, and this brought warmth and fertility; and in the west he sank to the underworld and brought blessings to departing things, like seeds, which were buried before they would arise in the new year. The north, where the sun never shone, was protected by the spirits of blackness. Somewhere in the west the sun entered the jaws of the earth dragon and went below the world, passing through the land of the dead, ruled over by Ah Puch, Lord of Death, who was depicted as a rather friendly skeleton. In the morning the sun rose from the other jaws of the dragon to spread light above the world again.

Fortune-telling   The gods were neither good nor bad in our sense, but classed as lucky or unlucky to mankind. The same god might bring blessings or cast his darts of destruction according to the season.

It was the same with people. They were born to be fortunate or unfortunate. Their nature was a matter of their fate, not of their fault, and if their fate led them to illness, accident, or mutilation, there was no thought of its being due to personal wickedness. If one crossed the path of a god at the wrong time, misfortune fell. This is not to say that the Maya were callous; they protected the unfortunate within the family and indeed considered that misfortune might show that the gods had a special interest in their victim. For people without homes or for suffering relatives, there was no hatred or disdain. The gods had visited them with affliction, and so they were given some assistance. It was thought very unlucky to refuse a handful of grain or a piece of cloth to one whom the passing of fate brought into one's life.

The reason for all this was that the Maya gods were not quite what we should call gods — that is, they were not independent beings, but really the great forces of nature. Nature is neither good nor evil. The Maya realized that they could not control wind or rain, nor could they decide when there would be a good harvest or a drought. So they accepted the fact that these forces were greater than the powers of mankind and made offerings to obtain the goodwill of the gods. The function of the priest was not only to make offerings to the gods and pray for good things in the name of the people, but also to find out the will of the gods and to forecast events. It is as if the priest were also the weather forecaster and the psychiatrist. In a tropical climate the regular changes of weather and the occasional big storms run to a fairly regular pattern of seasons. Priests worked out magic numbers which they could use to predict the regular comings and goings of the winds and rains (or of Kukulcan and Chac, as they named these gods). They also noted that the weather in each season of the year was marked by the regular movements of the stars through the sky. Thus there grew among the priests the idea that the stars and the weather were connected and that the gods on earth also had houses in the heavens. According to one

Forces of nature

25

Reconstruction of a Maya ceremonial center in a large city. The young astronomer-priest is sighting the horizon with his cross-staff, and the older priest is consulting astronomical information in his bark paper book. Late Classic styles

of the three magic books which survive from the ancient Maya, there were thirteen houses of the sky. Each one was marked by an animal shape among the stars. The animals symbolized the fate which would befall mankind when the star groups were rising on the horizon at sunset. They were all stars on the path which the sun traverses in the heavens, which we call the zodiac. In the tropical lands of the Maya this line passed right overhead at least twice a year, so it was easy to think of the stars pouring down gifts or shooting cruel darts as time went past.

At the great festivals the priests dressed as gods and *Festivals* performed wonderful dances, like the one painted at Bonampak, where the priests are shown in their fantastic masks and feathered robes moving up and down the narrow steps in front of a temple pyramid. The people must have thought that they were showing the actual dance of the gods among the stars in the sky.

The gods of things on earth were all nature spirits and were treated with ceremonies at the appropriate seasons. At the temple service in the summer the girls threw popcorn at the passersby. Later they went home dancing in processions, with their hair brushed down and breasts bare, rejoicing that the harvest was safely gathered in. The old priests, who had organized dozens of such annual festivals, must have looked on them much as we would regard the necessity to organize a team of harvesting combines to get the crops safely in. The Maya way was the more poetic and probably the happier because they were delighted that the corn-god had grown up and ripened. They believed that the goddess in the granary would bring her fertility magic to the grain they put in her care ready for the next planting. This would mean good crops next year too.

Of course, there were other gods, the spirits of war *Lesser gods* and of childbirth; of the passing moods of the mind, like sleep and waking; of the dance; and of hungry desire. People do not like to feel that these things come from inside themselves, and the Maya were very like the Greeks 27

Four gods shown in the Dresden Codex
(a) Itzamna as a wise old man
(b) Chac the rain-god with his thunder axe
(c) Kukulcan as the wind-god
(d) Ah Kan the corn-god

and other more advanced peoples when they decided that gods outside themselves conditioned human passions. Psychologists nowadays find out much of the causes of our behavior by studying our dreams, but the Maya thought that dreams were pictures sent to them by their gods.

Such were the gods of the Maya; not inventions, but natural forces revered and respected, because through them alone mankind could find life. The Maya developed their beliefs, with the help of their special gift for arithmetic, into a wonderfully complex way of foretelling the ways of fate, which mixed real science with their poetic adoration of the natural world. We shall look at this in the next chapter. It is the only way of understanding Maya dates and also the key to much of the meaning of their development of a unique kind of civilization.

Predictions   The ancient Maya differed from most other peoples by the importance they placed on the prediction of future events by studying the past. To judge by the few surviving books and the majority of the carved monuments, the Maya intellectuals were as obsessed by the study of horoscopes as the village farmers were absorbed in the cultivation of corn. But, of course, the farmers knew that they depended on counting time. They had to observe the festivals for the young corn-god and the rain festivals, as well as the happy harvest home celebration. Time united them all, and the priests watched the sun, moon and planets as they passed eternally among the stars. They realized that each day showed a different pattern in the sky, and assumed that each day must be some kind of god moving through the heavens. With him he would carry his load of blessings or sorrows, just like any Maya merchant traveling with his load of goods slung over his back from the strap around his forehead. After his day's travel the god rested, to resume his journey only twenty days later when his turn came again. As the Maya counted things in twenties (we have twenty fingers and toes, so the Maya word for twenty days was *uinal*, a man, all his fingers and toes), so they had twenty lords of the days who carried the burden of time, one for each day in sequence. Each of these twenty days had its own name.

They also gave numbers to days; these numbers were not 20, but 13. Why 13 was important we do not know, but there are 12 moons, plus part of a thirteenth moon, every year, so maybe 13 represented that side of nature. The Maya were also quite certain that one could not count time as one day until the first day was completed. So what we would count as the first day was called *Day Zero* by the Maya. Therefore, their 13 numbers for days ran from 0 to 12. Now, if you have patience, you can work it out and see that with 20 names for days and only 13 numbers to go with them, the first day, Imix, would be numbered 0, but in 20 days' time, when it came up again, it would have number 6 as its companion. You can go on working it out, and you will find that the first day becomes 0 again after 260 days.

There is no doubt that the Maya found this complex number game fascinating. As you see, it gives a period of 260 days, which they called a *tzolkin*. It was important for them because one's luck in life depended very much on which of the gods of the tzolkin days was controlling events on the day of one's birth.

The tzolkin doesn't fit the year, but the Maya, with a

real relish for numbers, had *two* kinds of year. They discovered very early, perhaps even before they began to think of themselves as the Maya, that the sun comes back to the same place among the stars; that the farmer must plant his corn at yearly intervals, 365 days apart; and that in every fourth year the sun is one place behind, so you have to count on another day as in a leap year. This natural year must have been of absolute importance in the daily life of the community. One must have a good solar calendar if one is to be a good farmer. Because it was so important they held a special celebration for the beginning of each *haab*, as they called the year.

The years and longer periods The haab is only rarely mentioned in the monuments, because the priests and magicians were interested in exact numerical time counts, and $365\frac{1}{4}$ days was not very useful to them. On the great monuments we find that they use a special count of 18 × 20 = 360 days, which they called a *tun*, meaning a stone. They put a stone on one side before the temple to mark this. As 18 was convenient for counting within a year, but otherwise of little interest, they went on counting by stages of 20. Twenty tuns were 1 *katun* – that is, 20 × 360 days. Twenty katuns were 1 *baktun* – that is, 20 × 20 × 360 = 144,000 days. So the baktun was 2,100 days less than 400 years. Twenty baktuns were 1 *pictun* of 2,880,000 days, or 7,885 years and 62 days. You can imagine what fun the astrologers had in working out the exact solar year anniversary of any date within the system of 360-day tuns. They were very exact about this, and often we find groups of dates, which we call distance numbers, in inscriptions, which have just this purpose of calculating the true solar anniversary of a date in the past or even of projecting it into the future. What magic was involved we do not know, but they were quite happy in occasionally calculating dates in multiples of more than 3,000,000 years into the past. There is rarely any error in their working.

The background of all this work was a theory. The Maya believed that each period of time had a god protecting it. Therefore, each time it recurred, the same kinds of gifts would be given by that god. All the different periods of time had their own rhythms, and so one could work out a very complicated group of influences affecting each day as it came to one out of the future. Would the crops fail this year? We must look up the magic records to find if the ruling powers will be against the corn-god. Will there be an earthquake? On what days were there earthquakes in the past? These will reveal when the earth jaguar is likely to be restive and shake the rocks above his lair. All events could recur, and one could predict them if one knew the rhythms of time. We can imagine the excuses the soothsayers made when things went wrong, but there remains no record to tell us.

In later times, after the breakup of the great civilization *Books of Chilan* of the cities of the old Maya, the new cities under Toltec *Balam* domination in Yucatán kept records known to us as the Books of Chilan Balam; these works were mainly prophecies, but were not as complicated as the earlier calculations. They assumed that each katun of 20 years in a sequence of 13 katuns would have the same kind of luck every time it came around. Thus, if there were 20 tuns of peace and prosperity, they would recur in about 260 years.

To add to the wonders of the system, the planets, like *Planets* the sun and the moon, were regarded as gods and goddesses. The sun moved across the sky according to the seasons, the moon changed its phases and was recorded very carefully as having two differing calendrical influences. The planet Venus was very important. Its cycle of change from morning star to evening star was recorded as a powerful influence on fate, and special significance was attached to the two periods when the planet was invisible from earth. Other planetary cycles have also been identified; Mercury, Mars, Jupiter, and probably Saturn, were known to the Maya astronomers, for they were in no point inferior in their observations to the astronomers of Babylon or Athens.

At the four corners of the sky stood the four Bacabs, the gods of the four directions. Each in turn ruled over 31 a 360-day tun. East, south, west and north made up the sequence, because that was the path of the sun through the sky. Very often the figures of these deities adorn the time-marker stelae which were erected each katun, and in particular at Copán we can identify them by their symbols. The god of the east is Kukulcan, wearing his quetzal bird (kukul) plumes. The south is ruled by a goddess wearing a skirt with jade beads all over it. The deity of the west wears a crown of plaited corn stems. That of the north shows a skull, for this is the direction where the sun is under the earth and is not seen by men.

Astronomy   The Maya priests made their exact astronomical observations from the platforms of the pyramidal mounds on which the temples were erected. They sat at the temple doorway and looked across a staff, held in their hand, to some known point; sometimes it was a wall of the temple, sometimes the crest of a distant temple seen on the horizon. This method gave them a direct line of sight in a fixed direction, and they could observe when the star they were watching passed the line. They could keep their calendar accurate by noting the exact time and direction in which stars crossed the horizon.

One must never assume that the Maya priests were just exact astronomical observers. They were really interested in the meaning of events seen in the stars and thought to influence happenings on earth. The fact that they could forecast solar and lunar eclipses and could date the rare transits of Venus really meant that they could prepare the proper sacrifices to the gods to avert calamities at these times. It was not just science for its own sake, but a public duty. The aim was to guide the people toward the fortunate days for planting and reaping and to have means of forecasting difficult times so that bad luck could be eased if not totally averted.

The sacred books   The painted books which were kept in the temple libraries contained a great deal of astrological lore. The beautiful Dresden Codex has one very special series showing the passage of the planet Venus through time, giving the

Maya Classic stela from Copán, representing the god of the west, wearing his
headdress of dried corn stalks

periods of visibility and invisibility quite exactly, and showing the different aspects of the power of the planet on earthly and heavenly levels. The planet was considered to have dangerous aspects, and the tables of its movements are accompanied by beautifully drawn pictures of the threatening spirits of the planet casting war darts against the various kinds of people who were to be afflicted with misfortune at these times.

To judge by the great artistic skill employed in painting it, this particular book must have been kept in an important temple. It may well be that these very complicated calculations of magic were known in detail only to the most important prophets in the priesthood.

Constellations In the Codex Peresianus, which, although much damaged, is as beautiful as the Dresden Codex, there is a long series of sky-bands decorated with symbols of the planets, and in thirteen sections we find a little sign rather like a pair of hanging leaves, one black and one white, and between them the glyph for Kin, the sun. These were the houses of the sun in the sky. Each is accompanied by an animal figure, and these animals are the constellations of stars in the zodiac. The pictures suggest that the Maya thought of the constellations as creatures dedicated to the gods, each of whom carried the sun through part of its path through the sky. This was roughly equivalent to the period in which each moon was in the sky. Each year contains twelve moons, plus another eleven days, so the Maya very sensibly allowed for thirteen groups of stars to guard the sun's path. Their

Drawing from Codex Peresianus showing two sections of the sky with the sun carried by various constellations: the water dragon, quetzal bird, scorpion, turtle, and rattlesnake

Carved limestone lintel from Yaxchilán (formerly Menche), showing a richly dressed priest carrying basket of sharp spines for drawing blood from his tongue as an offering to the god Kukulcan in the form of a serpent. Maya Classic

little picture symbol of the sun in its house between darkness and sunrise was quite natural to them, because their days began at sunset, not at midnight. Sun between darkness and light must mean sun on the horizon. And, of course, if you want to know which group of stars is on the sun's path on any day, the best thing to do is to wait until sunset, note where the sun goes down, and see which stars follow it. In the tropical latitudes of the Maya country the stars come out very soon after the sun has passed below the horizon.

Although those Maya priests may have put their astro-   35 nomical knowledge to a strange use, we must respect them as very practical people and very good observers. They worked out the exact length of the solar year a little more accurately than we do for practical purposes by adding our leap years. No wonder the Maya respected their priests and dressed them like the gods.

Priests and chiefs   We can see from the sculptures how wonderfully the priests were costumed, and we can learn something of their ceremonies. We can see how they offered their own blood to the gods by tearing their tongues with thorns and how they were dressed on great occasions in the sacred masks and glorious costumes of their deities. One gains the impression that among the Maya of the Formative and Classic periods the whole civilization was a theocracy. Perhaps, as in recent times, a Maya youth of good family began a career of public service by doing a minor job of work in the temple and then transferred to a civil post, rising alternately in religious and civil life until he became a leading priest, whereas nowadays he might become the city mayor. This system of advancement is so characteristic of the Maya that it may have been part of their way of life for all their history. Certainly it had great advantages, because the relationship between all phases of the power of the gods of nature and human life was better understood.

We know that in the times after the Toltec entry into Yucatán the power of the Maya cities was commanded by chiefs who were selected only from certain ruling families. It is almost certain that each city had its ruling family or clan in ancient times. At the time of the Spanish conquest there were conflicts going on among relatives of the Cocoms, the Xius, and the Itzás, who were the leading families in Yucatán, and it may well be that in Classic times, wars were caused by similar conflicts between the ruling families of the different towns. We think that for a time in the central area of the Petén around Tikal and Uaxactún there may have been some kind of confederation, since a group of towns adopted the same kind of lunar calendar and kept it for two or three centuries. Some of the sculptures show

36

Front of a carved step from Copán, showing a gathering of seated chiefs, probably astronomers. Maya Classic

gatherings of notables wearing symbols of different gods and seated on cushions which carry symbols that are rather like town names. It is apparently a gathering of notables from several towns in a kind of peaceful congress, possibly to settle astronomical problems.

The movement of the gods bearing time on their backs was important for the Maya, who not only regulated their farming year by this rhythm, but also made it the basis for their politics. For us, it means that we can date the curious horoscopes which they cast to guide them, and it also means that, except in very unusual cases, we shall not learn any history as we understand it. There may be a few names of city-states, perhaps also those of the war chiefs, the Nacoms, but little more, because where fate ruled, actual history seemed unimportant. For instance, there was a famine by decree of the gods, a war followed and the inimical gods were placated by sacrifice. According to the Maya prophecies, in 395 years we may expect a similar war, just as there were war and famine through the same gods at a similar period in the past. There is no other history in the world so strange and, to tell the truth, unhistorical as the Maya's.

History made of magic

37

CHAPTER THREE

The Classic Period of the Maya

Maya beginnings   MAYA civilization grew slowly at first. In the period which we call Formative, because Maya civilization was just beginning to take a definite form, the people lived in villages and made small temples on stone-faced earthen mounds. They seem to have been very like their neighbors, worshiping similar gods, particularly an earth goddess, whose little pottery images abound. Probably she was put in the fields to make the crops grow well, but we have no traditions from the Maya themselves to tell us this. Their beginnings are really mysterious.

Even the beginning of Maya writing is unknown. The earliest stone monuments copy the techniques of wood carving, so we conclude that they had wooden monuments with inscriptions before they put up the stone stelae which became so popular in their cities. Their time count for normal purposes began with Baktun 0, which would have been about 3800 BC, an unlikely date, because there was no trace of developed town life in any part of Middle America at that date. We come onto solid ground with two monuments in Baktun 8 – one at the ruined site of Uaxactún ("Eight Stone") which dates from the third century of the Christian era, and one from the great city of Tikal which takes the count back to about AD 80. In the core of a pyramid at Uaxactún, a still more ancient stone-faced pyramid was found; on it there were carvings of Maya masks in a style very close to that of the still earlier Olmecs of southern Mexico. At Tikal the old stela was associated with stone buildings and stone-lined tomb chambers which carbon datings put still earlier in time. A distinctive art style 38 was born even before the carved stone time-marker stelae.

An early Maya village with an artist making a clay figure from which his wife will make pottery copies

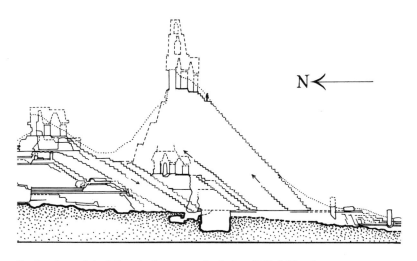

N←

Section through buildings in the great ruined city of Tikal. Note how one pyramid has been built up over another at different periods during the Maya Classic era

Early Classic   This world of the Maya in Baktun 8 was contemporary with the great period of Mexican civilization at Teotihuacán. Maybe there was contact through trade or war, but it was just about this time that the Maya cities also began to arise and grow beyond the scale of villages.

In the early centuries of the Christian era, the development of Maya cities was much more rapid. The carved stelae became common. At first the style reminds one of wood carving, but in the great southern center at Copan the carvings rapidly assumed the high relief which is characteristic of stone sculpture. Temples were being rebuilt constantly. Every katun a new skin was added to old temples, and with the enlargement came greater elaboration. Old sanctuaries were filled in carefully, and then new ones were made at a higher level to house the sacred images and costumes. The change from Formative to Classic Maya art has a short Preclassic stage, but really the development was surprisingly rapid. The earlier villages with temple mounds turned in three or four generations into great ceremonial centers with magnificent temples, courtyards

40

for the magic game Pok-ta-pok (see description of this game on p. 82), and even stone causeways adapted for processions. As at Tikal, some of these centers formed part of veritable cities with thousands of low mounds for houses around them. Other centers seem to have been simply holy places with only the necessary houses around them. The bulk of the population was spread out on the fields and plantations in the surrounding country, all of which was ruled by the priests and nobles who controlled the sacred central unit.

Classic arts

The true Classic period lasted three or four centuries. For much of the time the cities of the Petén region seem to have been either confederated or part of a unified "empire," but the outlying towns retained their special characters. The civilization was masterful and magnificent. Sculpture, pottery and writing all reached high degrees of perfection, even though no metals were used. From the sculptures we can seen the excellence of featherwork and weaving. From Tikal we have a few carved wooden lintels of the most excellent workmanship, all in low relief, but carved with grace of line and accuracy of level.

We have no histories of the Classic Maya period, but we can see that this was a rich civilization, in which there was time for people to escape from the eternal drudgery of gardening and hunting to get enough food to live. They had developed their skills so that they could obtain all their basic needs in about a third of the year, thus leaving plenty of time for communal work, such as building the great temples and enacting the elaborate ceremonial dances for the gods. There must have been a considerable number of specialist craftsmen among them. Their work in stone and wood is so splendid that it would be beyond the powers of craftsmen who had not devoted their life to learning their trade.

Women in art

Women, who usually do the weaving and make pottery in a primitive community, must have advanced to an important social position. Their work was as fine as anything ever made, although they were equipped simply with the

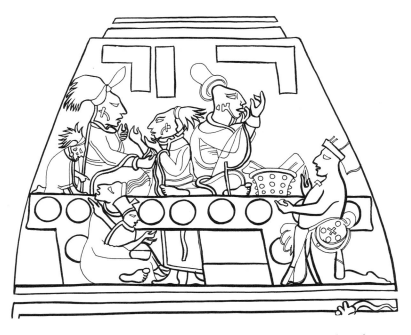

Part of the frescoes at Bonampak, showing the ladies of the court seated on a huge stone seat with a nurse holding a baby prince before a visiting chief

handloom and with no potter's wheel. Some of the sculptures show goddesses, and there are many of them in the painted books. At Bonampak we find a picture of a great lady who appears to be the wife of the Nacom, or war chief, and whose little son is held up before visiting nobles, presumably as a future chief. Similar ladies in tight-fitting shifts and with beads around their necks and wrists are found in the pottery figurines showing late Classic people from Yucatán.

Costume The costumes of important warriors and priests varied in style but were uniformly rich and brilliant. The basic garment was a long sash worn as a waistband and loincloth with pendant flaps in front and behind. These were sometimes embroidered. Fashionable men appear to have liked their waistband to be made of wide cloth rolled so as to appear like a thick belt about six inches deep. Sandals were worn, some with high ankle pieces almost like boots.

42

Some men wore capes, and these varied from a simple all-round shoulder cape to jaguarskins and sheets of featherwork worn hanging down the back. Headdresses were in immense variety, from elaborate feather war bonnets to crowns, inlaid with turquoise and shell, and to many kinds of turban, worn with rosettes of flowers and shells.

There was no metal jewelry in Classic times, for the good *Jewelry* reason that the Maya had no knowledge of metals. Their country had no resources of copper, silver, or gold. They wore red, purple, and white shells, sprays of feathers, and, most important, masses of green stones of various kinds, including a true jade. All hard green stones were considered powerful magic, and the Maya did not discriminate between jade and other green stones, although their preference for a cheerful apple green color led them to use the best of the local jades where possible. Sometimes we find deposits of jade buried in temples; they include some pieces in earlier styles, which must have been regarded as ancient heirlooms when buried.

In the new National Museum at Chapultepec in Mexico City, one may see the skeleton of a Maya priest found at Palenque. A slab of stone in the platform of the Temple of the Inscriptions was found to cover a staircase, which had been filled with blocks of stone. The Mexican archaeologist Alberto Ruz spent three seasons of excavation clearing this stairway. At the bottom his team of archaeologists and workmen found three skeletons guarding the entrance to a wonderfully sculptured burial vault; part of the flooring proved to be the lid of a sarcophagus containing the skeleton of a high priest or perhaps even the Halach Uinic, or great chief, of the ancient city. He wore a jade collar, wristlets, anklets, a skirt, a cape, and a headdress, as well as a wonderful mask, made of plaques of jade, which covered his face. Since the Maya used no money, we cannot guess the value of such a costume for a high priest. Its worth lay mainly in the travel needed to get the stone, the selection of the right stones, and the immense time taken by specialist craftsmen to pierce and cut this very hard material with no 43

The Temple of the Inscriptions at Palenque, with a section cut away to show how the grave of the high priest was set inside the foundation pyramid. Maya Classic

other tools than moistened canes dipped in quartz sand. Actually every one of the beads in the costume was polished into shape without the aid of any mechanical tools whatever.

Craftsmanship   Such finds as this prove to us that the Maya were indeed a rich people in their skill and patience, and that they showed good taste in making beautiful things. No semi-barbarous village craftsmen of the Stone Age could have made such a dress for their medicine man. This was the work of skilled craftsmen, well trained, who were working for the gods of a civilized city. Their gods were not just

44   barbarous images either, but were personifications of the

great powers of nature, not unlike the gods of the Greeks and Romans in the Old World.

All the splendor of the great leaders of the cities was devoted to religion. It appears that for great ceremonies the chiefs held court, and the priests performed their ceremonies and magical dances on the open stairways of the temples and in the ranges of small rooms which surrounded temple courtyards. In the temples themselves, on the top of the pyramids, the rooms were small and very dark. They must have held divine images and stores of costumes for gods and priests and must have been the places where victims were offered up after public sacrifice on the open front of the pyramids.

Sacrifices

The Maya appear to have performed human sacrifice only rarely. There was a rainmaking ceremony in which a victim was thrown down from a scaffold onto a heap of stones, and sometimes dwarfs were sacrificed to avert the evils of eclipses. Maybe there were more blood offerings than we know, but on the whole the evidence is that the Maya were never as bloodthirsty as the Mexican Aztecs in matters of religion. They were much more likely to offer their gods presents of food and flowers, and when it was necessary to offer pain for the good of the people, the priests tore their own tongues with thorns in order to offer blood and anguish to appease the powers of nature.

Ceremonies and priests

The larger city centers in Classic Maya times were a complex of courtyards surrounded by several kinds of stepped pyramids, themselves often mounted on a bigger staged platform, like mountains rising from a plateau. They were wonderful constructions for their purpose of a religious ceremonial performed in the open before the whole population of the town. Only the secret offerings made before the holy images, which the people probably never saw at all, were made in the god houses. We do not know if the people really believed that the priest wearing the mask of a god was the divine being in person. It *is* possible. However, it is probable that the priest wearing the mask felt that the spirit of the god had entered into him.

45

Left Cross section of an interior wall at Copán showing the rubble hearting.
Right Detail and cross section of a façade at Kabah in Puuc style showing how the stones were fitted into a rubble and cement hearting

Even today the inspired dancers in some West Indian ceremonies feel that a spirit has entered their bodies and they act and speak like some other person. Certainly the Maya knew a great deal about this kind of hypnotic trance.

Building work As we have said, the temples were rebuilt by having a new building piled over the old one every katun of 360 × 20 days. What was inside the mound hardly mattered. In a few cases, like the high priest's tomb in Palenque, a passage was left open through the whole series of buildings as they were erected. Mostly the cores of buildings were of rough rubble and earth, with a facing of stone, which grew thicker as each new layer was put on. In some cities a burnt limestone cement was used for holding the stones of the new building firmly in place over the old one. The facing stones were ground down to fit like big building bricks. It was well done and orderly, with regular rows of stones all of the same thickness. Where carving was made, it was cut into the finished wall and ran right across the joints in the stones so that the carving looked like a continuous design, not like one made up of rectangular blocks. In other cases, notably at Palenque, the stone walls were often coated with a cement rather like stucco and were smoothly molded with beautifully flowing patterns of figures of the gods among plants and trees.

Although the Maya were good at calculations, they never *Arches* worked out the geometry of a true arch, like the one the Romans adopted and made the basis of most of their big buildings. When the Maya wanted to bridge over a space with stone, they used a corbeled arch – that is, they put slabs of stone on top of the walls, and then layer after layer of slabs were arranged so that each layer projected inward over the space to be covered just a little more than the layer below it, rather like an inverted flight of steps. When the two sides came close enough to be covered with a cap-stone, the masons trimmed the edges clean so that the corbeling looked like smooth upward pointing curves, not like inverted flights of steps.

Maya corbeled arches: *left* a trefoil arch from the palace at Palenque, and *right* a pointed arch from the upper story of Las Monjas at Chichén Itzá

 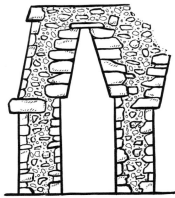

47

Wall decorations   Nearly every interior wall in a Maya building was covered with a thin layer of plaster and painted, or else it was lined with sculptured stone slabs. In many cases the narrow dark rooms could have been used only by people carrying torches, but the elaborate decoration was there just the same. Alas, a thousand years of damp tropical air has in nearly all cases crumbled the plaster and destroyed the paint! Luckily at Bonampak the heavy rains dissolved the limestone from the roof blocks and covered the paintings with a coating of stalactite. Thus a great deal of them were preserved until colored copies could be made. This was a single small building; what we have lost from the more important cities is only to be imagined. Their gorgeous colors and vivid sense of decoration must have made them among the wonders of the world.

Painting   Much of our knowledge of Maya costume and ceremony comes from their painted pottery, which followed the same artistic tradition as their wall paintings, but which unhappily was limited to the few colors which can be used on pottery meant for daily use. But with this to guide us, in conjunction with sculptures, jewelry, and the few surviving painted books, we know very well how the Maya appeared in their great days and how splendid were the buildings of their heyday.

Changes of style   We owe a great deal to the Maya habit of putting new coats on ancient buildings. The layers of old structures are often much damaged, but they give us plenty of evidence of the growth of architecture and the changes in artistic taste. Maya art is a unity within a series of regular changes. It had no sudden break away from its steady stream of development until after the fall of the ancient cities of the Classic period. One may compare it to the slow change and development of Gothic art in Europe over four or five centuries. It is the same with all manifestations of art; the steady development followed the same path in sculpture, pottery, painting, jewelry, and writing. All individual city-states apparently vied with one another in keeping abreast of new designs. In the central Petén, where we find
48

the period of calendrical uniformity (see p. 36), there remain individual local differences of detail, but the development of style follows the general pattern of all the Maya cities. It shows that whatever the nature of the wars, one of which is painted at Bonampak, there was a continuous exchange of ideas. Probably this was conducted by bands of traders going from one place to another, but it is also possible, indeed likely, that there were pilgrimages to one or other of the great cities dedicated to some special deities. For instance, Quiriguá has nearly all its great stelae carved with the feathered plumes of Kukulkan, whom the Mexicans knew as Quetzalcoatl, and was probably specially dedicated to him. This pilgrim trade could explain why we find some cities produced thousands of molded pottery figurines of gods and noblemen.

The Maya left us few definite records of their social life *Social life* in ancient times. We know from a few paintings and from sculptures and pottery figurines that women were accorded a fair position in society and that they had their special spheres of work. They held a well-defined position in the home and were probably always very busy. It is true that the labor of getting up in the early morning to grind the cornmeal for the family food for the day was heavy work and that there was little rest in a woman's life. Even when the women were walking to market, they were always busily employed twirling their weighted spindles to make cotton thread. However, what would have happened if a man had tried to grind corn or to spin thread is impossible to imagine. It would be an act so much opposed to the Maya ideas of right and wrong that the offender would probably have been killed to prevent disaster from falling on the community. Similarly, a woman would not have dreamed of using a digging stick in the ground. The husband would thrust the stick into the ground for planting the corn grains, and the wife would come up behind him to cover them over with a sweep of her foot and to arrange the hillock for them to germinate. The man would burn down brushwood and chop the trees on the plantation, and the 49 woman would expect to watch over the growing crops. Men would make spears and paint books, and women would do the beautiful weaving and would coil pots, although many special pots must have been painted by men who knew the magic of the pictures of the gods. It all was so arranged that each member of the family had a recognized place and helped the family without making any confusion.

Children   The children had the best of all worlds among the Maya. They were free to play and were much fussed over and petted. They were not often slapped, and it was considered bad to make a child cry, unless it was at some ceremony for the rain-gods, when tears would make them send the rain from the skies. There were toys, like balls and dolls, to play with. Sweets took the form of especially nice fruits and popcorn dipped in honey. But most of the time of the children was spent imitating their parents. Thus they learned about grown-up life without trouble.

An ordinary child living in a village had little to learn beyond how to keep house, how to farm, and how to keep lucky by going to the temple ceremonies and watching out on unlucky days. But for the child of a village headman, life meant more, because somewhere within the family there might be the next headman, and it might be himself, so he had to be wise in the ways of people and learn early to serve the village. Responsible children had begun to take some simple public office, like sweeping the temple courtyards or leading groups of dancers, by the time they were twelve.

Governors   Probably each city in Classic times was governed by a ruling family. On the whole, the leading families among the Maya seem to have prided themselves on being good governors, who ensured the well-being of their people by good administration and successful magic. These families would be closer than other people in descent from the gods, or perhaps have seized power in some past wars. The families were really widely scattered clans. The Nacom, or war leader, would not always be succeeded by his son or nephew; sometimes a distant relative might be selected

50

Seated nobleman, with cotton headdress. Pottery. Maya Classic

as best for the job by the family council. The real governor of a city was the Halach Uinic, who inherited his position as the favorite son of the previous chief. He was never a despot, but ruled his town with the advice of a council of elders, warriors and people with a reputation for practical good sense. It was not easy to become a member of the ruling group if one was not in the family, but occasionally great warriors were invited. All the offices were usually shared by the selected members of the ruling family. The war leader was equivalent to the high priest, and the civil leader, who was a judge, balanced a leader responsible for community affairs.

One learns, in the later Maya annals, of strategies and treacheries which indicate that political considerations entered into the quest for power. The evidence of changes of rule and wars in the older Classic times, especially the period of calendrical uniformity in several cities of the Petén area, suggests that even then there were movements for increasing the power of one group of rulers over those of other towns, but there are no details from which we can really study the process of political development in Maya history.

Noblemen   The Maya no doubt held their rulers in great esteem. One sees from the Bonampak frescoes that the Halach Uinic and his wife were people of great dignity. They were surrounded by officials who wore splendid costumes and headdresses which presumably denote their rank. If costumes are anything to go by, the Nacoms, or war leaders, were less important than the priests, who were dressed as gods and can sometimes be seen speaking from behind the masks of the gods. It seems that in the Classic period of the Maya, people were governed by nobles who were mostly interested in the search for the will of the gods through the regular observation of time and the rituals of the temples. No doubt they exercised great political power and struggled within their caste for greater positions, but the business of administration and war was probably delegated to functionaries of social grades a little lower than that of the Halach Uinic, who was mediator between the Maya and their gods.

Artists   The abundance of magnificent works of art testifies to the existence of a highly trained group of artists. It is probable that their work was regarded as a kind of religious office, especially since the object of all art was to present the gods and the powers of nature to the understanding of men.

All works of art were made under a very strict series of rules, and each part of a figure had its approved proportions; but at the height of the Classic period the Maya were quite near realistic representational art. They kept some formalities of posture, with the head usually in profile and the feet turned to one side, but this artistic convention was less marked than in Egyptian art. The Maya even standardized the symbols used for ornament – for example, the special ornamental patterns which referred to the planet Venus or the wavy structure representing corn leaves – but the artists used these standard forms so well that they achieved the appearance of naturalism.

The painter was as important as the sculptor, although he was probably not an equal of the lapidary who worked 52 hard jade. The painter's range of colors was limited to

Maya classic stela representing the goddess of the south, wearing her jaguarskin skirt covered with jade beads. From Copán

natural dyes and colored earths, like ochers. The outlines of figures were always drawn in, usually in black, and the details filled with solid color. There were probably many more kinds of painting than we shall ever know – for instance, painting on furniture and cloth hangings. All we have now are a few wall decorations, the finest remains of which come from Bonampak, and some good Classic fragments of writing and decorative design from walls at Palenque. These show a controlled skill in the use of a brush which may be compared to the work of a competent signwriter of today. Such technical ability in the freehand drawing of curves and the deliberate variation from thick to thin line are evidence of a long period of training.

The painted books   There are three painted books of the Maya still in existence, but they all belong to a period after the abandonment of the great cities of the forest. The older two are known as Codex Peresianus and the Dresden Codex. Codex Peresianus is much worn and damaged by age and is extremely delicate. It is, however, very beautifully executed and of considerable scientific importance because it includes a list of the groups of stars of the zodiac. The even lines and the clearness of the glyphs are perfect.

The Dresden Codex, like all other Maya books, was made from a long strip of bark paper, which, according to tradition, was strengthened by addition of a paste made from pulped agave leaves. This was then painted over with limewash and was finally written on with black ink and watercolors, mostly red, blue and yellow. The document is very detailed, giving an immense amount of information about time counts and the relationships of the different gods to one another. It shows many more figures than the Peresianus, and these again have great delicacy of line. Their outlines are so full of curls and scrolls that we can compare them to the more fantastic works of Baroque design in Europe or of Javanese art in Asia. The lines are wonderfully even, but very thin. Alas, we have no clue to the kind of instrument which the Maya artist used as a pen!

There can be no doubt that both these documents belong

to a truly Maya culture without a Mexican influence, although in the Dresden Codex the time counts in the calendar appear to date from the eleventh century, at a time when the ancient Maya cities had been abandoned and the Mexican Toltecs were lording it over the newer northern cities of the Maya from their capital at Chichén Itzá.

Away to the north of the Petén forests lies the great *Yucatán* limestone plateau of Yucatán. Water is obtained from the natural wells formed where underground limestone passages have caved in, allowing access to underground streams. However, this limitation did not deter the Maya of the Classic period. They had learned in their highland cities, such as the great metropolis at Tikal, to construct rainwater conservation basins lined with fine cement to prevent seepage. The problems of life in a country without surface water were familiar to them.

The Maya tribes of the Yucatán Peninsula apparently built most of their important towns in the latter part of the Classic Maya period. Monuments in them date from the fourth to the tenth century. At the beginning of the tenth century there was a break in continuity and a sudden falling off in the quality of workmanship. We know that at this period the Maya of the cities in the Petén region ceased to build and apparently left their homes altogether. We do not know the reason for this disaster to Maya civilization, but it was less intense in Yucatán than elsewhere.

There were differences of style which were very important *Yucatec arts* when the early cities of Yucatán are compared with the other Classic sites. On the whole we find evidence of a different social structure in the abundance of elaborate corridor types of buildings with many small dark rooms opening off the top areas of long terraces ascended by steps. These appear to have been palaces in which the nobles could live, at least on ceremonial occasions. The cool dark rooms must have been a relief from the glare of the sun on white limestone, and the habit of sitting on low benches did not demand high rooms. At the far end of every court-

The palace of the governor, at Uxmal, Yucatán. Chenes style of architecture

yard was a great temple pyramid, always showing that the gods were greatest among the nobles. Perhaps the most wonderful of these Yucatec pyramids is *El Adivino*, the house of the "magician-prophet," at Uxmal in Central Yucatán. The temple on top of the pyramid was covered with a geometric series of sculptures, building up to an enormous formal dragon mask, which, when colored, must have looked like a wonderful Turkish rug.

Puuc style   In the Puuc cities of northern Yucatán the tendency is for the lower parts of walls to be decorated with patterns like carved wooden posts making up the sides of a house, and then above them an elaborate mosaic of carved stones, in which one finds symbols of the sun, the wind serpent, the planets, and over and over again the strange long-nosed mask of Chac, the rain-god. In the limestone plateau all life depended on rain, rather than on the rivers, which were all underground. Naturally Chac was revered as the most important of the gods of this world.

No doubt the differences in architecture represent different tribal groups of Maya who controlled the areas. Probably the Chenes style, with its great temples representing the mouth of the great earth dragon, was related to some distant Mexican ideas, and the fact that in later times the Xiu family were lords of Uxmal is probably enough for us to assume that among the intensely traditional Maya there was some Mexican influence in the days before the catastrophe in the tenth century. The name of the post-Toltec rulers, the Xius, indicates that they worshipped the fire-god who was the Mexican equivalent of the Maya's Itzamna, in that he was the earthly manifestation of the supreme creator. Tradition said that the Xius arrived in southern Yucatán in the year 869 and moved little until the Itzá invasions. They are said to have settled at Uxmal when Ah Zuitok was their Tutul Xiu, or high chief, as late as 1007. But whatever remnant of population survived from the ancient inhabitants of Uxmal was probably receptive to the ideas of the new settlers, who brought a great chiefly tradition with them. Actually one is always aware of cultural contacts between the Maya and the Mexican peoples. There was never any time when the trade routes into Yucatán and Guatemala were abandoned, and the Maya were by nature interested in trade. *Chenes style*

There were Classic sites all round the coast as well as in the central areas of Yucatán. We know that in later times Cortes stayed with a Maya chief whose trading canoes traveled right around the Yucatán Peninsula. There is no reason to suppose that it was very different in ancient times. On the west coast there were important towns at Chakanpotun (present-day Champotón), Campeche, and Jaina. On the north coast only small trading posts led inward from fishing grounds to the great cities. On the east coast there were Isla de las Mujeres, Cancuén, Cozumel and Tuluum. They were probably all centers of local chiefs *Coastal towns*

57

through the centuries, because they were natural trading posts. At the island of Jaina there was a very special local trade in pottery figurines of the gods. These are beautifully made figures, cast in molds and colored. They were traded widely, and when first discovered at other sites, they were often suspected of being forgeries because of the delicacy and realism of their style. In their own way they are the equivalent of the naturalistic figure painting of Bonampak, and represented a powerful trend towards realism in Classic Maya art.

Yucatec books and painting The longest of all the Maya painted books is the Codex Troano-Cortesianus, now in Madrid. It was apparently made shortly before the Spanish conquest of Yucatán. The work is coarse, compared to the two earlier works, but its drawings have a wonderful life and activity. The scribe used at least two sizes of pen, so that he often had thick outlines in his writing, with thinner inside details. The book deals with agricultural life, giving pictures of the four New Year festivals, the ritual planting of corn, and details of fortunate days for hunting or for weaving.

These few books and wall paintings are all that remain to us of a great artistic tradition in painting, which lasted for more than 1,000 years.

One might think that the many sculptures would tell us more, but their story is only a partial one because originally all the sculptures were painted. There is a little evidence remaining in traces of color in crevices in the monuments, but so far none of the Maya Classic monuments has been reconstructed in colored casts. There is a reconstruction of part of the wall of a building from Chichén Itzá which has been made as near the original as humanly possible, but this brilliant exhibit in the British Museum is almost totally Toltec in style, even though it shows Maya warriors among the Toltecs.

The colored monuments of the Classic cities of the Maya must have been fantastically beautiful, although we might find the prevalent use of a dark mulberry red, bottle green, and deep blue was violently in contrast with the bright

Group of Maya pottery
(A) Early Classic from Tikal, showing Mexican influence from Teotihuacán
(B) Classic polychrome pottery from Guatemala
(C) Plumbate trade vase from Yucatán
(D) Fine orange ware dish, Toltec period, from Chichén Itzá

yellows and sky blue. But one must remember that the tropical climate and vivid light of the Maya area made these very rich colors much more pleasing to the eye than they are in temperate latitudes.

Maya pottery was made mostly by the housewives. The simple domestic wares are often of excellent shape. No wheel was used to throw the shapes, but the pots were made from coils of clay welded together by hand. The potter helped herself by using the kabal, a block of wood which she slowly turned with her feet while modeling

Pottery

59

the pot by hand. The pots were made from local clays, which were usually mixed with a little sand or crushed limestone. They are even in thickness, and sometimes small vessels are quite thin, although the system of firing in a pile of burning wood made the resulting earthenware rather soft and a little crumbly, so that it was necessary to keep the walls of any big pot on the thick side.

Pottery decoration has immense variety. Some pots were decorated by being stamped with seals pressed into the clay; some were painted red and yellow with fine paints which filled up the pores in the earthenware. Others were baked in a pit and covered with leaves to make them come out a fine, even black color. The finest of all pots were painted with figures of gods and priests, in red, yellow and brown with black outlines. This painting is so expertly done, sometimes with hieroglyphs painted on it, that we must guess that these pots were for religious use and were painted by priests trained for this specialist work.

Figurines   In some of the Maya cities there was a very large output of little pottery images of gods and people. They were usually made in clay molds in two halves which were stuck together with soft clay before firing. Usually the back was plain, except for a whistle built into its base. Did you call a god by blowing the whistle? Was it simply a toy? Was it made as a musical instrument to be blown in a series of rhythmic notes in an orchestra? We do not know, but we are sure that these excellently designed little things were important in Maya life because of the great numbers which were made. At some places, like the island of Jaina, there seem to have been a group of specialist manufacturers of these pottery figurines who had brought their craftsmanship to the level of an art form.

Metalwork   The Maya had no metalworkers until the invading Toltecs brought in goldsmiths and bronze casters from Mexico. There was no metal in the Maya country, and all the finds of metal treasures from the sacred cenote (see p. 86) at Chichén Itzá have no truly Maya designs among them. For the rest there is a single gold bell from Palenque, which may have been made from a generally Maya design by some goldworker from the south, perhaps from Panama.

As we have noted, the Maya found their need for jewelry satisfied by the possession of fine stones like jade, crystal, and masses of shell beads and pendants. The glittering robes and headdresses of tropical bird feathers must have amply compensated for the absence of gold and silver.

Weaving was highly regarded. A few fragments of cloth *Weaving* have been found, but the wet climate destroyed most of the textiles in which Maya notables were buried. However, the pottery figurines tell us that the belts and loincloths of the men and the shifts worn by the women were made with an eye to fashion, and the paintings show that they were often colored and embroidered. Many of the sculptured monuments show elaborately decorated garments, beautifully made in a style which looks like damask. One suspects that they were woven by specialists and were not the usual garments woven by mother and daughters in the home, though among the modern Maya men take a good part of the weaving on themselves, and it is possible that in ancient times the more elaborate and wider pieces of cloth were woven by men.

Bark paper was used for books and for ornaments such as elaborate headdresses. However, cloth was woven from homegrown cotton, which was produced in great quantities, sufficient for visitors to note that when walking from one village to another, the Maya women were always spinning their cotton thread. We know that they had a good knowledge of vegetable dyes and so could make brilliant tapestry with dyed thread, but we have no specimen to see. The poorer people sometimes wore garments made of henequen fiber, which must have been like a finer variety of the same material which we now use as sisal rope.

Leatherworkers could cure skins of deer, leopard and *The end of the* serpent. We find all these materials depicted on paintings *Classic period* and sculpture. One supposes that they were used by the costume makers in the temples and palaces, as well as by the family at home.

When we think of all this, we can see that the Maya of the Classic period could live a very rich life. There was little to disturb them as long as their fields produced corn and cotton, and the forests were populated by birds and animals. The cities were beautiful, and the temples were constantly being enlarged. The climate must have been reasonably comfortable, and there is every evidence that trade, carried by large groups of porters with packs on their backs, was a feature of everyday life. The Maya of this older period must have been a civilized and efficient people, living in comfort and contentment. The desertion of magnificent temple precincts and even great cities like Tikal, which in the seventh century must have been more populous than any European city except perhaps Byzantium, could not have been without reason. There were earthquakes which cracked some of the temples before the final exodus, but no city was totally destroyed. Otherwise we have no solid facts on which to base our theories about the fall of the old Maya cities. The only clue is the history of parallel events in Mexico at the time of the destruction of the Toltec empire.

The Toltecs   The Toltecs (see p. 77) had been ruled by a noble clan descended from a leader thought to have been an incarnation of the god Quetzalcoatl. Soon after 990 they suffered catastrophe. It arose from the last high chief's choosing to appoint the son of a beautiful concubine to be his successor. The four nations that made up the Toltec empire revolted and then started fighting among themselves. The last prince, Naxcit Quetzalcoatl, escaped apparently by sea to Yucatán. Mexico was partly depopulated by the war, and a pestilence that followed decimated the Toltecs. It is said that even two centuries later only twenty noble Toltec families remained in the Valley of Mexico.

The fall of the older Maya   It is possible that there was also a terrible outbreak of pestilence among the Maya, although the last known date in the older Maya style is equivalent to AD 909, long before the wars in Mexico. There can have been no direct link between the two events. Certainly the Maya population

A Toltec chief, from Chichén Itzá, with the serpent symbol of
his god Quetzalcoatl (or Kukulcan)

63

in Yucatán seems to have survived in much weakened numbers, unable to resist their new Toltec overlords. There may well have been, as J. Eric S. Thompson suggests, a revolt against the old tradition of semidivine priest-rulers. This would account for the almost total abandonment of ancient buildings.

But we also have to reckon with the possibility of climatic change. It was in the tenth century that the climate of the present-day southwestern United States became dry, and the old agricultural tribes there were driven to take refuge in fortified towns on the mesas because of hunger-driven invasions by wild hunters from the plains. It may well be that this same climatic swing brought the tropical rain belt farther north than formerly and increased the jungle growth so much that it was hardly worthwhile for the Maya farmers who had survived the other catastrophes to combat the forest. The change left the Maya of the great forest terribly broken up. They seem to have rebuilt a civilization on a much smaller scale. However, after the further catastrophes of the Spanish conquest, the survivors of the Maya in the great forest became the ancestors of a gentle people, known to us as the Lacandones, who still worship in the ruined temples of their forefathers on ceremonial occasions, but they are otherwise seminomadic forest hunters. They appear never to have tried to build up cities, but left that kind of social effort to their cousins, the Quiché of Guatemala – who seem to have been half-Mexican anyhow. The Quiché, however, had nothing to do with the mixed cities under Toltec rule from Chichén Itzá on the limestone plateau of Yucatán.

CHAPTER FOUR

Maya Writing

THE most remarkable thing about the Maya civilization is its development of a system of phonetic writing. Most of the American peoples had some system of pictorial writing. The Toltecs, and the Aztecs following them, used a system of writing the names of people and places by drawing symbols of things which would make up the syllables of a word when their names were pronounced. A good example is the ancient name for Mexico City, Tenochtitlán, which was written as a block on which are a stone and a cactus. One read this by using the *te* of *tepetl* ("stone"), the *noch* of *nochtli* ("cactus"), and *titlan* ("beside"), shown by the block shape supporting the glyph. The name read Tenochtitlán in the Nahuatl language, but it may also be read in English as "Beside Cactus Rock", which is a true translation of the name of the city. *Mexican writing*

The Maya went far beyond this level of writing. They used nearly 700 characters. Many of them were once pictures of objects, like feathers, jewels, or the heads of birds and animals. But in the course of time the pictures became formal patterns, of whose origin we cannot always be sure. Every sign, or *glyph* as it is called, is surrounded by a line, except for a series of prefixes and suffixes, which are left outside the line that encloses the main glyph. *Maya glyphs*

This knowledge is quite recent. In the past there was a deep mystery about Maya writing. The first man to take an interest in the written language of the Maya was Diego de Landa, who was the missionary Bishop of Yucatán soon after the Spanish conquest. He knew nothing of the ancient cities in the forest or of long inscriptions on monuments. His concern was with the strange books which the Maya *Bishop Landa*

BAKTUN
400 Tun

KATUN
20 Tun

TUN
360 Days

UINAL
20 Days

KIN
Day

POP

UO

ZIP

ZOTZ

TZEC

XUL

YAXKIN

MOL

CHEN

YAX

ZAC

CEH

MAC

KANKIN

MUAN

PAX

KAYAB

CUMHU

Maya calendar glyphs for long periods of time and for the twenty-day months

Part of the Late Maya Codex Troano-Cortesianus, showing hieroglyphic writing and women spinning and weaving. (The last one is the death goddess)

used to keep records of their religious ceremonies and to foretell the future. The good bishop was pleased that his new children were clever enough to have a system of writing, but he was appalled at the religious ceremonies described. He felt sure that many of these things must have been inspired by Satan. So while he was trying to learn about the way the Maya wrote, he was also seeking out the religious books to destroy them. In this way he was only doing what the Maya themselves did during intercity wars. However, he wrote so sternly against these evil and idolatrous books that he earned the reputation of the man who destroyed Maya literature. That is not quite true. He certainly made a ceremonial bonfire of nine great books and encouraged other Spaniards to hunt out more, but he did not destroy the history books which we know as the Books of Chilan Balam. These were preserved for a few generations after the Spanish conquest, when they were rewritten by the Maya themselves in the Spanish alphabet, which they found easier to use than their old style symbols for nearly 700 syllables.

Reading the *Maya books* Bishop Landa discussed the whole question of the Maya calendar very thoroughly with the local wise men. They gave enough information to enable him to describe the simplified system of the katun count. He also made rather hurried, but still decipherable, little drawings of the signs which they used for the names of days and months. When Landa's book was rediscovered in the nineteenth century and published by the Abbé Brasseur de Bourbourg in 1864, it became possible to read Maya dates and to move a little beyond Landa by using the Maya systems of numbers to find larger units of time. There was, however, only a hazy correlation with the Christian calendar, and it took a long time for three or four different systems of correlation to be evolved. The solution was approached seventy years ago by F. Ducane Goodman and later confirmed with small corrections by the Mexican scholar Dr. Martínez-Hernández and the English researcher J. Eric S. Thompson.

The result of the kind hearted compromise made by the Maya was that when archaeologists attempted to read the inscriptions, no one could make anything of them. It is true that much ingenuity produced an account of the destruction of the kingdom of Atlantis from the Codex Troano-Cortesianus, but it was certainly not what the Maya had written in this book. Considerable progress was made in studies of the three remaining religious books by American, British and German scholars. It became possible to read syllables connected with the calendar when the sequence of dates suggested their meaning. Similarly, from their associations with time, it was possible to identify the main signs for the directions and for colors.

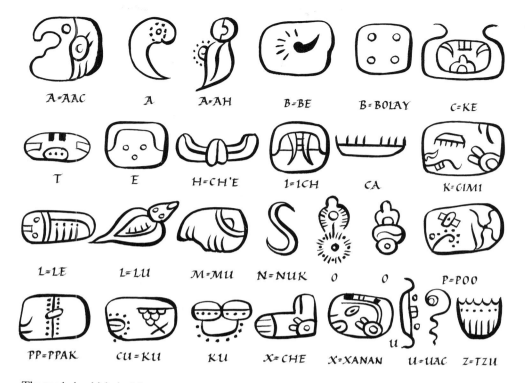

The symbols which the Maya gave to Bishop Landa when he asked them to draw an alphabet for him

The final steps were the publication of the large volume, *Maya Hieroglyphic Writing*, by J. Eric S. Thompson, which classified and compared the known glyphs in a reasoned system; the similar classification on a formal plan by Günter Zimmermann and Thomas Barthel in Germany; and the work of Yuri Knorozov in Russia. Knorozov was not a Maya specialist, but a scientist interested in the general development of writing from the pictographic stage to phonetic symbols. His work on the Easter Island writing was parallel to the more complete German study, but in the Maya field he reached the conclusion that the development of syllables must follow the same plan which had occurred elsewhere in human history. He expected to find a 69 grouping of sounds and determinative symbols, which were used to show what class of thing was meant by the sound. With a good Maya dictionary and the known calendrical glyphs, Knorozov was able to identify most of the symbols in Bishop Landa's "alphabet" as being based on syllables. Once this had been done, it was possible to go ahead and spell out phrases in Maya and find syllables which had not been previously identified.

The problem of decipherment

The work of decipherment is not finally settled. It is clear that a great many extra syllables can be read and that whole phrases can be found. A preliminary translation of most of the Maya documents has been published by Dr. Knorozov. His system is not yet the perfect answer, and American scholars have been able to improve and correct parts of it, but it is clear that the Maya hieroglyphs can now be read. No doubt the next century will see many adjustments and corrections. We must expect that to happen, because the same occurred in the century and a half after the Egyptian hieroglyphs were first translated. But we can be sure that the general contents of the Maya books can now be understood.

What does the new knowledge reveal? Simply that the Maya were more interested in the good and bad fortunes associated with the counting of time than in recording history. One special pleasure, however, awaits us, and that is to know the names of the wonderful cities in the forest as they were spoken by their inhabitants long ago.

How the Maya wrote words

In Maya writing the method of arrangement of syllables to make up a word is quite complex. Landa's book gives us the word *elele* written as two pairs of symbols. But when we apply the new system to it, we find that we spell out *e-lu-le-e-lu-le*. The sounds have to be abbreviated to *e-l-l-e-e-l-l-e* and then contracted. It is strangely parallel to Mykenean Greek, in which syllables are extended for each sound in almost the same way. Landa's second example was a short sentence, *Ma in Kati*. It was written with signs which read *Ma ich-nuk Kab-ti*. Once again, under the same principle of contracting the syllables, *ich-nuk* becomes *i-n*.

70

The system is very complicated to our eyes, but it is apparently a natural one used by many peoples when they first discovered the art of writing.

In any case one can understand how the Maya grasped the idea when they were asked to make an alphabet for Landa. Landa's open vowel *A* sounded to them like their glyph for *Aac* and another one for *Ah,* so they gave him both glyphs. The sign for *Ppen,* a slave, did duty for *P,* and *K* was expressed by the skull, which was the sign for the day Cimi. When it came to spelling out the word *A-ha,* they used two signs which read *Aac-Ha;* but since *Aac* was the turtle, they added a special sign showing that the turtle's head was only part of the whole creature. At first glance one expects a third sound to be there, but it is really just to clarify the glyph for Aac. It is probably best to get a good Maya grammar before one tries one's hand at deciphering a text. Better still, let the specialists read the inscriptions and then dispute over their results until they agree what the reading should be.

A further complication to the subject is that we know *Changes in* very well that the Maya language has changed a good deal *language* since the Spaniards first heard it spoken in Yucatán. To the modern Maya the language which Landa recorded was an old-fashioned Yucatec dialect. When we deal with the monuments from the cities in the forest, we must realize that the inscriptions were written from 6 centuries to more than 1,000 years before the coming of the Spaniards. We can expect a good deal of difference in this dialect from that spoken in 1520. The difference may well be as great as that between Anglo-Saxon and contemporary English. In addition, we are not sure which of the many dialects of Maya was the one spoken in the great cities of the Petén region. It appears now that it was closely related to Chol, as J. Eric S. Thompson suggested sometime ago. In fact, it is only in the last year or two that all the varied ideas about Maya writing have begun to fall into place, and it has become clear that there was a good deal of truth in many things which formerly seemed irreconcilable.

We may be fairly certain that the Maya learned the art of writing from their neighbors, the Olmecs and Zapotecs, but they adapted the idea and introduced many symbols which can have meaning only in their own language. In other words, once they had the idea, they set to work to make a truly Maya system of writing, and carried it forward to a far more advanced level than any other people on the American continent.

Who could write? There is not the slightest reason for thinking that every citizen among the Maya could read and write. The glyphs are many and very complicated; they have one form when carved in wood or stone and a variant form when written or painted. To use them properly would have demanded a much longer period of training than we have when we learn alphabetic reading and writing.

We may be sure that the power of writing belonged to the Maya priests and rulers, who alone could provide sufficient leisure for their younger members to learn the art. As we have seen, the inscriptions are mostly to do with religion and more often than not have long calendrical calculations involved. They were made at the orders of highly specialized priestly magicians, presumably the rulers of the wonderful ceremonial cities.

When the old system of government collapsed and the great temples were deserted, the art of writing was not lost. Short historical annals were written, first in Maya and later in the Spanish alphabet. Religious books were painted, such as those seen by Bishop Landa, which were almost certainly like the Codex Troano-Cortesianus, now in Madrid. This is not as elegantly drawn as the earlier works, but its simplicity allowed the scribe to write in a strong uncomplicated style, which is still readable by those who know the more elegant older styles. The final stage comes in the debased, but still just readable, glyphs which were drawn by Bishop Landa. It is quite clear that Maya writing was in decline by 1520 and that it was time for them to learn a simpler system, like the alphabet, if their

knowledge was to be preserved.

CHAPTER FIVE

Maya and Toltec:
A Changing World

ONE after another, the great Maya cities ceased to erect monuments at the beginning of the tenth century. The decline was not always a prelude to total abandonment. In some places, temples badly scarred by earthquakes had been patched up, and simple stone rooms fitted into the ruins. However, none of the older Maya cities survived as active centers of any importance.

In Yucatán the story is very different. The Maya had *Yucatán* lived there in small towns. Inscriptions, such as a dated monument from Tuluum, tell us that the Yucatec Maya made monuments dedicated to the gods of time at least as early as the fifth century. Probably the limestone shelf which constitutes the Yucatán Peninsula was even drier in ancient times than it is now, so that the communities were small and confined to two areas: the seashores and the water holes where the limestone had fallen through into caverns, thus providing natural wells, called cenotes, which opened onto underground rivers.

The Maya towns in Yucatán developed their own styles *The new Maya* of architecture, sometimes using columns. The Maya there *towns* preferred to erect buildings with long corridors opening into many small rooms. A whole building was often decorated with a relief pattern, almost like a vast embroidery. This was achieved by carving portions of the design on each of the stone building blocks and fitting them together like a mosaic. We call their architecture the Puuc style, and very attractive it must have been when painted in vivid color to set off the designs on the white background.

Legend tells us that the people were ruled by families *The rulers* of nobles, who controlled the military organization, pro-

Front of a palace at Sayil, Yucatán, showing Puuc style of architecture

vided the priesthood from among themselves, and exacted a tribute from the farmers to keep the whole organization going. It may be that the older cities in the forests were ruled in the same way, but we have no proof. We hear of one great Maya family of this type, the Cocoms, who were later engaged in asserting their power over the cities controlled by the Mexican warrior clans, the Xius and Itzás.

The different life of the Yucatec Maya On the whole, it seems that the Yucatec Maya, living in more open country and with their great ceremonial centers adapted for use as dwellings, as well as temples, were much more involved in political life than in religious ceremonial.

Quite naturally the Yucatec Maya were interested in water supply. Their country had no surface streams, even in good times, so they were interested in the protection of the great cenotes from which each town drew its water and in the regularity of the rains which fertilized their crops. Many of their buildings were covered by designs representing the strange long-nosed mask of their rain-god, Chac.

74 Since the Yucatec cities used the Maya calendar and

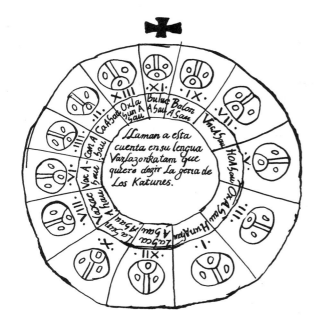

A Maya
katun wheel from
a Book of Chilan
Balam. Post-
Conquest work

wrote inscriptions in the typical Maya hieroglyphs, we
may be sure that they had plenty of contact with the cities
of the forest, even in the days of their decline. Apparently
the Puuc cities lost a great deal of their importance about
the time of the desertion of the forest cities, but their later
recovery may have been due partly to an improvement in
the rainfall or to an increase of population by a migration
of people. We cannot tell. It is most probable that if any
migration from the forest did take place, it was of the
plebeian population, for we have no real evidence for the
survival of the old calendar dating system in Yucatán. It was
sufficient for the Yucatec to count in rounds of 13 numbered
katuns, so that their longest unit of time was 13 × 20 ×
360 days = 256 years, less 30 days (roughly 1 moon). For
all practical and historical purposes this katun round was
quite sufficient. These farmers and administrators were not
concerned to keep long astronomical records in order to
calculate the effect on the present of astrological happenings
thousands of years ago.

*The Yucatec
calendar*

75

The Tutul Xiu (head of the Xiu clan of the Toltecs) dancing a war dance. His rank is shown by the bluebird at the front of his headdress. From a wall painting at Chichén Itzá

Costume Judging from the few representations of people in the Postclassic period, the costume was basically the same as that seen on the ancient monuments of the forest cities, although it was much simpler in style. Yet the very decorativeness of palace façades presupposes a textile art as rich as that which once produced the embroideries and tapestries depicted on the lintels from Yaxchilán in the Petén. There had been a change, but not a total destruction of the past. In Old World terms, it was much the kind of alteration which took place between the times of imperial Rome and the new Roman empire of Charlemagne.

History All the Maya histories deal with the Yucatán Peninsula. They are mixed with prophecy and magic, but they do suggest that there had been longstanding contacts between Yucatán and Mexico before the arrival of the Toltec nobles, who organized an empire and rebuilt the small, but ancient, city of Chichén Itzá. The suggestion in the histories is that the Xius (Xiuh is a Nahuatl word meaning fire) were an important force within the Maya area before the arrival of the Itzás. This is indeed very likely since we know from Mexican legendary history that in the times of Quetzalcoatl (that is when the Toltec rulers took the title of their god) the Mexicans had enjoyed a world in which all kinds of imported treasures were available in quantity. These included vanilla and chocolate, as well as tropical feathers, so one may be certain that trade was extensive and included the Maya lands.

Even in the highlands of Guatemala, where the Quiché Maya ruled after the failure of the cities in the forest, there was a sacred collection of Maya legends, the Popol Vuh, which is thoroughly Mexican in type, just substituting Quiché names for the Nahuatl ones. The beginnings of the new period of Maya history were as closely linked with the Toltecs of Tula in central Mexico as the beginnings of the Classic period of the Maya were linked with the people of Teotihuacán, also in the same central region of the Mexican highlands.

The story seems to be one of a curious link between the two nations at a time of destructive crisis. The civilization of Teotihuacán had been destroyed by AD 550. After a century it was replaced by a group of military conquerors, the Toltecs, who established an empire, which they expanded in regular planned raids to reduce the whole of Mexico to obedience. The rulers of the Toltecs regarded themselves as descendants of the god Quetzalcoatl (who, as we have said, was the same as the Maya god Kukulcan). Near the end of the tenth century there was a collapse. A civil war broke out, bands of warriors fought each other, and then a pestilence broke out. This event was at least eighty years after the closure of the Maya cities in the forests.

Golden eye and mouth mask, with symbols of Quetzalcoatl (Kukulcan), dredged from the Cenote of Sacrifice at Chichén Itzá

Cocoms and Xius

In those days Yucatán seems to have had two important ruling families: the Cocoms, who were truly Maya, and the Xius, who were at least partly Toltec. The ruling family of the Toltecs, led by Naxcit Quetzalcoatl, followed the legendary path of their god and took ship for the sunrise – that is to say, they paddled from some point on the Mexican Gulf Coast for Yucatán. Once in Yucatán, they were accepted as great lords and eventually occupied the then small city of Chichén Itzá, which they made the center of a new Toltec empire. Their city was architecturally Mexican, not Maya, and was even more splendid than fallen Tula. However, these Mexicans were very close to the Maya and rapidly learned to use Maya writing. Their art and architecture influenced the surrounding Maya cities but did not make them anything like Toltec in their spirit. Apparently Maya soon became the general language. As has been shown, throughout their later history the Maya were a people who absorbed foreign contacts and were never themselves absorbed.

We may be quite sure there was social change, since the Toltecs, who had a king descended from Quetzalcoatl at their head, were interested in dynastic conquests, rather than in ritual magic. Their cities, both in Mexico and in Yucatán, were secular cities with palaces, buildings dedicated to the warrior orders, and comparatively few temple pyramids. The all-embracing religious unity was gone from Maya art, and at Chichén Itzá we have frescoes and reliefs of warriors; even the deities are costumed as Toltec warrior chiefs. The change is similar to the social changes which occurred in the European Bronze Age, when the cattle-pen earthworks and great stone monuments of the early Bronze Age were replaced by the great defensive earthworks and mighty swords of the middle Bronze Age.

From the very beginning we find Maya symbols in Chichén Itzá. It is clear that the magnificent ceremonial center had Maya sculptors and masons at work on it. They were probably working under Toltec designers, and among them local Maya specialist carvers had enough priestly training to know something of hieroglyphic symbolism. However, the mass of the architectural ornament was strictly Toltec in style, and the same applies to what remains of figures of the gods. This makes it certain that among the settlers were a group of highly specialized Toltec priests who could at least mark out the figures on the blocks of stone and who in all probability produced some of the carvings themselves. Similarly, the remains of fresco painting show the use of the typical Maya techniques, which after all were common to most of middle American wall painting, but are almost completely Toltec in design. The naturalistic tendencies of Classic Maya art were totally lost, apart from some interesting scratchings on walls. What replaced them was a highly symbolic method of presentation, which simulated naturalism but was made up of symbolic figures, much as one composes letters to make a page of a book.

The earlier sculptured walls at Chichén Itzá were masterpieces in their way. Time has destroyed much of the painted surface, but careful restoration of a section on a plaster cast in the British Museum has shown that the fabulous stories of the artistic achievements of the Toltecs were not all imagined. One of the chief values of these works of art is that they depict different groups of people, bringing Maya nobles among the Toltec chiefs. They are evidence of the new mixed culture which arose in Chichén Itzá. That it was to be taken over by the Maya was not then apparent, for the Maya seem to have been regarded as a nobility themselves – deprived however of the priceless asset, the right to rule inherited through Toltec descent from the divine Quetzalcoatl.

Tuluum A truly Maya city, on the west coast of Yucatán, is Tuluum. Although it contains an ancient stela dated in the seventh century, most of its existing buildings belong to a rather severe variant of the Puuc style. They are well proportioned and are either rectangular flat-roofed rooms on low mounds or large platforms on pyramids approached by stairways which led to a temple room on top. There were often smaller rooms below at the ends of the main plinth. The masonry is well constructed and in many places has been overlaid with cement. The site, beside a rocky bay facing the Caribbean, is beautiful. It is not easy to approach from the sea, but its situation would make it a useful trading point for coastal canoe-borne merchandise.

In one of the temples there remains a section of a wall fresco painted with severe good taste in black and blue, with figures of gods and a sacred tree. It is interesting to note that here the costume has altered a good deal from the older Maya dress and that it has much closer affinities with Toltec clothing. In particular the goddesses wear a short cape very like the Mexican *quechquemitl*. The painting, however, retains a good many features akin to the Maya painted books. It is not so hurried as the Codex Troano-Cortesianus nor so elegant as the Dresden Codex, but it has affinities with both. However, this painting is truly representative of the Maya style of the period soon after the development of a Toltec dictatorship centered upon Chichén Itzá.

Farther south at a site known as Santa Rita, Dr. Thomas

Gann unearthed a fresco painting on a wall surface buried in a mound. This showed Maya deities in a thoroughly mixed style with many Mexican influences, but the figures were accompanied by katun date symbols in the true Maya style. The quality of the work is worthy of the Maya Classic, but the curious angularity of the figures and the use of the katun count make it quite clear that this is another late Maya style of painting showing Toltec influences.

Throughout Yucatán we find that pottery does not reach *Late Maya* the high standards of the Maya Classic art. A few vessels *pottery* are of a high quality but are so much of Toltec design that they may be recognized as Mexican trade wares. Most of the local pots are gray ware, and they include a number of grotesque, roughly made figurines. These, however, have a remarkable vitality and look like caricatures which could come to life at any moment. Many of them had once been painted over with limewash to fill the pores and had then been painted in brilliant color. They must have been attractive objects in their time, but now that the coloring has powdered away and only the gray clay is visible, one can see the roughness of the modeling and the lack of care in their manufacture. Of course, a great deal of this may be due to the lack of good potters' clay in Yucatán. Pottery was supplemented by shells and wooden vessels for many purposes, but little of this work remains.

There can be no doubt that the Yucatec Maya were very *Wood carving* good craftsmen in wood. Many wooden objects are shown in sculpture and painting. We also know of the remarkable dugout canoe with a crew of forty men which Christopher Columbus encountered off the Bay Islands. He noted its size, its excellent quality, and the use of fine awnings of colored cotton as a protection for the principal merchant and the cargo. These Maya traders were astute enough to persuade the Admiral to travel away from their country, and so saved their people for a few more years of independence. Perhaps the boat came from Tuluum or perhaps from some seaport nearer the Bay Islands, but there can be little doubt that it was Maya and that it impressed even 81 the old sea dog Columbus, who must have seen all the European craft of his day and known what to look for in good boat design.

One cannot expect to have any knowledge of the state of minor arts in the times before history caught up with the Maya because the climate is not suitable for the preservation of perishable objects. Not even a single feather cloak or fan has survived to tell us of the fine workmanship and splendid appearance which is alluded to by the Spaniards who saw them in use. No doubt they were less elaborate than the great feathered headdresses of earlier times, but nevertheless they were made in quantity for use on ceremonial occasions.

The first use of rubber One of the most remarkable products of southern Mexico and the Maya country was obtained from a small tropical tree, *Castilloa elastica*. This was rubber. The trees were tapped, and the latex was smoked as it had been for unknown centuries, even before Classic times. The rubber was used, unpredictably, as an incense to the rain-gods, because the black clouds of smoke looked like storm clouds bringing the desired fertilizing rain. It was also used for waterproofing capes made of palm leaves, a custom which the Spaniards did not adopt until a century after the conquest of Tayasal, the last independent Maya town on Lake Péten-Itzá in the Petén district, which fell in 1697.

The ball game The most popular use for rubber was in the sacred ball game called Pok-ta-Pok. The balls were solid rubber and four to six inches in diameter. They were heavy, and in a fast game a blow from one of them could easily be fatal. When the white men saw rubber balls bouncing for the first time, they thought that there was a demon in the ball that made it jump. It was certainly wonderfully different from the leather balls filled with feathers which used in Europe in those days.

The Maya molded the balls of rubber for a competitive game which had some magical connection with the movements of the planets in the sky. They played in a specially built court shaped like a capital letter I, with high walls

82

Left A hand carrying a throwing stick, modeled on a wood base, in natural rubber. From the Cenote of Sacrifice at Chichén Itzá

Right Ballplayer wearing hip pad. Pottery figurine. Maya Classic

around it. In the middle of each of the long walls a stone ring, with a hole in the center just big enough for the ball to pass through easily, projected from the side, high above the ground. The court was marked out into four quarters, each representing one of the four directions. The first team of players tried to keep the ball among themselves and prevent the other side from gaining control of it. Sometimes a team made an outright win by getting the ball through one of the rings high up on the ball court wall. This might do very well for players who could use hands or feet, but Pok-ta-Pok was played without using either for striking the ball. The blow on the ball had to be delivered by a leather pad strapped to each player's hips. The players wore helmets to protect their heads. One hand was padded with a thick leather glove, with which to strike the ground as the players hit at the ball.

83

It needed long practice and remarkable agility to become a distinguished player at Pok-ta-Pok, but the frequency and size of the ball courts in Maya sites show that it was an important game. Actually it was a kind of religious spectacle. The ball represented the sun among the stars, or the variation of fate moving from one quarter to another and from one kind of directing force to another. The whole thing was symbolic. In the unlikely event of the ball's being passed through one of the goal rings, the winning team had a claim to any jewelry they could take from the spectators. Fortune had smiled for them, and they were greatly honored.

The game was associated with sacrifice, but it is by no means certain whether the Maya often made a human offering to the spirit of the ball game. The game was ancient among them, possibly even earlier than among the highland peoples of Mexico. In fact, it could hardly have developed anywhere except in the tropical habitat of *Castilloa elastica,* because the rubber ball was an essential part of the element of chance in the game.

One suspects that there were significant differences between the game played in the smaller open courts at Copán in ancient times and the Mexican variation played between the enormous vertical walls of the largest of the ball courts at Chichén Itzá.

The decline of the Toltecs   As time went on and the Maya gradually regained control of their country, the Toltec influences in art and culture declined, but they had radically altered things. Never, after the coming of the Toltecs, was the old magical Long Count of time used in astrology; never again were the temples to be greater than the palaces of the nobles; never again were great stones erected to mark the passing of the katuns. The period of change was sudden. What the catastrophe of the old civilization amounted to we cannot fully judge, but only a poor shadow survived to grow strong again after the period of Toltec domination. The new Maya culture was as separatist and as full of local loyalty as the ancient, but it was oriented in new ways which were perhaps not truly Maya.

CHAPTER SIX

The Maya in Yucatán

THERE is no record of the details of the Itzá conquest of *The Itzá*
Yucatán. The Books of Chilan Balam describe the Itzá
people as one of a group of clans of Mexican origin that had
earlier contacts with the Maya. They had moved up the
west coast of the peninsula and entered the limestone
plateau sometime before they were able to make Chichén
Itzá into the great city from which they dominated the whole
land. We are sure that there were trading contacts with
various peoples in Mexico throughout all the history of the
Maya, but it was only after the collapse of the Classic Maya
civilization and the abandonment of the cities in the forest
that the Mexican Toltec empire collapsed. The Itzás who
founded Chichén Itzá and made it another, more glorious
version of the old Toltec capital of Tollán were themselves
refugees. They were driven by a religion which made them
certain that, as descendants of the god Quetzalcoatl, they had
a divine right to rule. The god under his Maya name,
Kukulcan, was already well known to the Maya. However,
the reasons for the completeness of the Mexican conquest of
Yucatán were probably their greater ferocity in war and their
long experience in ruling the centralized Toltec state which
had collected forced tribute from its subsidiaries.

Chichén Itzá had a very special claim on the Maya people; *The sacred*
among its cenotes it possessed one which was the sacred *cenote*
home of the water spirits. This natural circular pit, with
deep water at the bottom, was known to the Maya from
olden times, but to the Toltec Itzás it had a far richer
significance. Their tribal god, Quetzalcoatl, was shown in
the magic books as making offerings of incense and jewels
at just such a sacred well, in the distant past. The Toltecs 85

The Cenote of Sacrifice at Chichén Itzá

Human sacrifice built a temple beside the sacred well, just outside the main complex of fine city temples and palaces, and there the priests performed the great ceremonies to bring rain and avert drought. Five centuries later, when Chichén Itzá was no longer an important place, Bishop Landa was told of the sacrifices but was given a rather confused tale. He was informed that when they desired rain, the priests took girls who with other victims were cast from the temple over the clifflike sides of the great cenote. They had been selected in infancy for their beauty and had been brought up to be sacrificed. He reported that they were thrown in alive, and the people believed they did not die, even though they never saw them again. However, in some cases bodies floated and were then taken out and buried by the priests.

86

Both Maya and Toltec chiefs took part in the gorgeous ceremonies held in Chichén Itzá, but the power was effectively in the hands of the Quetzalcoatl chief of the Toltec rulers.

As time went on, another city became prominent. This was Mayapán. The name is a hybrid one, for the *Maya* refers to the speakers of Maya, and the *apan* part was Nahuatl. The mixture apparently means *"at the place of the Maya"*. There was tension between the two cities, but Chichén Itzá kept control because it was the center of the Quetzalcoatl of the Toltecs and its power was considered a divine right.

Mayapán

However, within Chichén Itzá there was a struggle for control of the city. An ambitious chieftain from Mayapán, named Hunnac Ceel, planned a seizure of power by playing on the superstitions of the people. At the great rain ceremony he arranged to be thrown into the cenote as one of the victims. He must have been thrown clear of the stones near the edge and have dived successfully. Three days passed, and on the fourth Hunnac Ceel reappeared with a message from the rain-god. One guesses that he had hidden among debris and rocks and breathed through a cane or tube of some kind. However, having been returned alive from the mysterious other world, he was regarded as a prophet. He used his power to install his clan in positions of power and eventually had himself appointed as ruler. Alas, Hunnac Ceel was not worthy of the Toltec tradition and used his power to satisfy personal grudges! He had rival chiefs seized, degraded and tortured. He extracted unfair tributes and aroused such anger and unrest that revolt might well have occurred.

The treachery of Hunnac Ceel

At last the treachery of Hunnac Ceel was unmasked, and war broke out. Chichén Itzá was overthrown, and Mayapán became the dominant city. It is a strange place. Even today the ruins look poor and shabby, even though they are surrounded by a defensive wall of great strength. Mayapán was the only walled city in that part of the world. Within the city there is another walled enclosure where there are ruins of rather poor palaces and undistinguished pyramid temples. The whole place is divided into small enclosed areas. The histories tell us that Mayapán was the center of an empire of sorts and that the eldest sons of the Maya and Toltec lords of subject towns were compelled to live there.

Maya independence

Mayapán lasted for nearly four centuries. It had no real center of power, and as subject towns rebelled, it became less and less able to hold its position. The Xiu warriors finally helped the Maya to break up the League of Mayapán and to drive the last Itzás into exile, but there remained no central authority which all the peoples of Yucatán would obey. For the last century before the Spanish conquest the Maya towns were independent of one another. They were under the rule of different noble families, who tended to form loose confederations with cities ruled by their relatives. The organization was weak, and wars were frequent. The Maya culture of Yucatán had inherited a great past but had lost the ability to profit by it.

Books of Chilan Balam

Throughout all the period of Toltec domination in Yucatán, records had been kept. These form parts of the Books of Chilan Balam. Apparently each town once had its chronicle. These are not straight history but, as their names indicate, are basically books of prophecy. It appears that in some ways they were poor descendants of the great magic works of the Classic Maya. However, the Maya had lost their long astronomical calculations and no longer worried to list lucky days for the religious ceremonies. In the seventeenth-century form in which they have come down to us, the books give us the fortunes associated with each of the sequence of the 260-day tuns as they fell in order within the U Kalay Katunob – the counting of the katuns. The day-to-day calendar simply lists whether a day is lucky or unlucky.

Some of the books give descriptions of the kinds of events which will happen in each year. Wild animals will attack the cornfields, or there will be a bountiful harvest, or one should expect a stormy year. The ancient tradition

88

of this kind of prophetic book had survived, although much detail had been lost. It had in fact become simplified to the level of the Mexican style of prognostication, although one is aware that the Mexicans had further knowledge of magical procedure which did not find its way into the popular books of the fortune-tellers. Apparently the Maya formed much more closely integrated communities than the Mexicans, and knowledge was more easily disseminated.

The Codex Troano-Cortesianus is a pre-Spanish book of the Yucatec Maya and is full of information on weaving, hunting, planting, the proper New Year ceremonies, lucky days, and so on. It is not made in a very elegant style and does not represent a highly cultured community. In fact, one may almost call it a villagers' almanac. Yet, although it was not from a college of priests, it contains much more of the world of charms and magic than any Mexican book. Presumably it belonged to the priests of some small town who were much concerned with the events of daily life. It gives us, therefore, closer contact with the people for whom it was intended than the earlier Maya codices, which are full of most wonderful calendrical calculations and were meant for the wise Maya priests of the period of Toltec domination. It is utterly different from the sculptured panels and stelae of the Classic period, both in its lack of elegance and in its direct simplicity. It is a nice simple magic book rather than a treatise in theoretical astrology.

Village life in a Maya book

At times it is almost a jolly document because the artist has seen all the things he depicts in daily village life. The people who have been around him are his gods and goddesses, but they have been adorned with the special symbols of the deities they represent. The goddesses wear their hair long and black, and dressed in a topless skirt, they sit or kneel on the ground to work at looms suspended from rough branches of trees. The gods use fire sticks, or throw their darts just as the men of the town do. These later Maya have not the sense of the mystery of the great powers of nature which their ancestors displayed in their art. The social slide has led to a kind of near equality, in which honor is marked by position within the village council rather than by feathered robes and intellectual achievements.

The new Maya towns
This is the kind of thing one would expect to arise after the Toltec episode. The invaders had made themselves like gods and had depressed the local chiefs. When the invading culture had drifted into impotence, it had dragged down the level of local chiefs. When the revolt came and the Maya regained their independence, there was a whole social organization to be rebuilt. The old leading families survived as village chiefs, and some of them were town chiefs; but there was only disunity and jealousy. The histories tell of a continual process of quarrels and separation. Alliances were made to destroy a rival city; but once it was defeated, the alliances broke up, and perhaps the defeated city even took over some of the former allies and used the new grouping to defeat its conqueror.

Bishop Landa tell us of their markets, their busy households, and their attachment to the old gods, but he makes it clear that his beloved Maya were not so nice as he would like to think they were. He tells us that they held festivals for the gods only with the intention of getting favors from them. Sacrifices were only made when they felt that the gods were dangerously angry. He is pleased about this because he found the Maya were much less aggressive and bloodthirsty than the Mexicans. But he goes on to say that human sacrifices were made in every town at one time or another, usually when the priest, or Chilan, thought it best. These sacrifices were made in public in front of the temples, and all the people agreed with the priests that it was necessary for the public well-being.

Towns in the forest
At the other end of the Maya country, which seems never to have come under the domination of Chichén Itzá, there remained a more truly Maya kind of civilization. Hernando Cortes has left us his account of how he traversed the land route through the thick forests of the Petén. Before he left the swamplands of the Gulf of Mexico he met a Maya town chief who controlled a great trading business.

Loads of seaborne merchandise were taken from the Coat-

A high priest wearing the stone knife headdress of the Itzá sacrifices a young man to the serpent form of Quetzalcoatl (Kukulcan). From a wall painting at Chichén Itzá

zacoalcos region by canoe right around the Yucatán Penin-sula to the region of the Bay Islands and Honduras. The one chief was in contact with his fleet of trading boats and received regular reports of events. He was able to draw a map for Cortes which showed the whole peninsula with such accuracy that the Spaniards were able to use it to find their way by the overland trails. In at least one place Cortes was able to direct a march by setting his compass bearings to the lines on the map.

In the journey across the Petén the Spaniards found some Maya towns and noted that most of the chiefs lived in fine wooden houses. In one case Cortes was impressed by a large and airy hall which a chief used as his council chamber. In two places on the route he found towns with large pyramidal temples, and in one he was impressed by the broad paved tracks, the big central square, and the array of many temple pyramids. These were not the great cities of the Classic period, or more recent explorers would have found traces of the later buildings among the ruins; but they represented a new Maya culture, which had risen in the same area as the old. The names of villages and some-times of chiefs show that the Mexican influence was present here. The towns were well organized, and the people seem to have given faithful service to their chiefs, even deserting and burning their towns if the chiefs told them to do so in order to avoid the dreaded Spanish conquerors. The main point to notice is that the towns and cities were in dense forest country and were often cut off from one another, although there were a few paths kept open for trade. But there was no question of any grouping of towns under a central control. Communications were too bad.

The town of Chacujal The most important town the Spaniards saw was on a trade route by canoe to the Gulf of Honduras. It stood near the Polochic River in Guatemala and was named Chacujal. Cortes found the place deserted, and when, eventually, some of the local people were found, the Spaniards had some difficulty in understanding them. Cortes says that he had to communicate by signs and a few words of the language he knew. Presumably these townsfolk were speaking the Pokonchi dialect of Maya. Cortes tells us – or, rather, told the emperor to whom he was writing –

"I gave orders to my men to keep well together, and marching through the place arrived at a great square, where they had their temples and houses of worship; and as we saw these temples and the buildings around them just in the manner and form of those of Culhua Mexico we were more overawed and astonished than we had been hitherto, since nowhere since we had left Aculan (on the Gulf Coast side of the Maya country) had we seen such signs of policy and power".

He went on to tell of great supplies of provisions in the houses which had suddenly been deserted by the Indians. He listed corn, cacao, beans, pepper, salt, fowls, pheasants,

92

Drawing of a Late Maya wooden palace as described by Cortes

partridges, edible dogs, and a great deal of cotton and "linen" cloth, and he mentioned plantations around the town. Later, having made friends with a few Indians who had returned to the town, Cortes was conducted to the river. The Spaniards marched two leagues (about six miles or ten kilometers) through fine orchards full of cacao and other fruit trees. Fom this point they were told they would reach a confluence of rivers in five days and would then come out into the Izabal Lake.

The town of Chacujal was not near any marked site of Classic Maya cities. A ridge of mountains separated it from ancient Quiriguá, sacred to Kukulcan. We have every reason to believe that Chacujal was a Maya development in the forest lands and was built after the catastrophe of the early tenth century. Modern discoveries in the ruin field of ancient Tikal show that 1,000 years earlier than Chacujal it had the same arrangement of a fine ceremonial center, surrounded by town houses and then miles of plantations. 93

No doubt rumors of the terrible events which culminated in the Spanish conquest of Mexico had reached Chacujal from traders; hence the precipitate flight of the populace, covered by a light rearguard action against the Spanish-Mexican scouts. The difficulty of language showed that the local people were neither Yucatec Maya nor Mexicans of the type of the Itzás.

The Late Maya
people
A special point of interest is that the people of Chacujal used longbows for fighting and hunting. No such weapon is known in the Classic Maya sculptures, and as this was the first contact of the Pokonchis with the Spaniards, we must assume that they had learned to use the bow from some neighboring peoples to the south. It may well be that the descendants of these late Maya of the forest regions are among the present-day Lacandones, a gentle and almost extinct group of Maya who worship the old gods, wear long cotton gowns, and, unlike the Maya of the Classic era, use the bow and arrow.

We must conclude that the last days of full Maya independence saw a surviving group of truly Maya tradition, living in villages and a few towns in the great forests. They appear to have been slowly developing their contacts through trade routes following forest trails and river transport. But they were radically different from the other Maya peoples of the sixteenth century.

In the mountains of Guatemala and southern Mexico there were Quiché and Cakchiquel Maya, who, according to their religious books, were largely of Mexican descent and were a successful ruling class among an indigenous population that had been easily subdued.

Civil wars in
Yucatán
In Yucatán the Maya cities were newly escaped from the yoke of invading Toltec groups such as the Itzás ("People of the Stone Knife") and the Xius ("Fire People"). Their civilization was brilliant, but not deep. Constant tension between ruling clans led to wars in which no single group and no central city showed any sign of emergence as a dominating power. The state of dynastic war, which probably existed throughout all Maya history, had become

94

Toltec and Maya warriors. The Toltec chief, the Tutul Xiu, has the serpent of Quetzalcoatl flying over him. From a golden plaque from the Cenote of Sacrifice at Chichén Itzá

much more violent and cruel because of the traditions imported by the Toltec invaders. The sense of military honor and the accumulation of skulls as trophies for public display in the forecourts of the temples were not truly Maya characteristics, but belonged rather to the code of honor of the northern Indians of the great prairies. It is hard to believe that the Spanish conquest of Yucatán imposed any new hardship on the native people, who had been too often exposed to the burning of cities and to massacres in intercity wars.

On the whole the Maya accepted Spanish domination quickly, although some heroic dissidents were still able to preserve their indepencence until 1697 in the Petén district at Tayasal on Lake Petén-Itzá. However, as the name denotes, these were people of largely Itzá descent, who followed a brave northern tradition which was not truly of Maya origin.

The Spanish invasion

95

CHAPTER SEVEN

The Maya and the Spaniards

First contacts THE first contacts between Maya and Spaniards were not friendly. In 1511 the survivors of a shipwreck took to a boat, and nineteen of them reached land in Yucatán. The local chief seized them, and four were immediately sacrificed and eaten. The others were unappetizingly thin after their ordeal in the open boat. They were penned up and well fed in readiness for a sacrificial meal, but they were exchanged as gifts with another chief. Most of them died from ill treatment and improper diet. But two survived, having been traded to a chief who was interested in them and gave them hospitality. They were very well thought of by the Maya. One of them survived to be picked up by Hernando Cortes in 1518 on his way to Mexico. The other married the daughter of the friendly chief and became a high official among the Maya, accepting their ways and remaining faithful to them so that when offered a chance to return to his own people, he simply sent messengers to say that he was not interested. However, the first unfortunate meeting gave the white men their first name among the Maya. They were the *Men Who Ate Custard-Apples;* this sounds all right until one realizes it is as good as saying *the men who are so primitive that they eat pig food.*

The first account   There may have been other shipwrecked mariners of
of the Maya whom we know nothing at all, but in 1510 the Spanish navigators Juan Diaz de Solís and Vicente Yáñez Pinzón made a trading voyage. On their return to Spain they gave an account of their voyage, together with a map, to Pietro Martire d'Anghiera. This was printed in Pietro Martire's work *Decades of the New World* in 1511. However, Solís and Pinzón gave false sailing directions, substituting south

96

for north. Their story gives accounts of trading and fighting at a number of named Maya towns and even gives the titles of Maya chiefs whom the navigators visited. Trade was not always welcomed, but if one chief attacked the visitors and drove them away, the next would welcome them and establish a market. When the map was printed by Pietro Martire, it showed the whole coast of Mexico, from Yucatán right around to Florida, before it had been officially discovered. It is sad to relate that this voyage probably brought the infection which killed many thousands of Maya citizens in 1515 and 1516. The descriptions sound like an acute form of smallpox. But because no one in those days knew the causes of epidemic diseases, smallpox was taken as a terrible visitation of the gods and not blamed entirely on the visitors.

The Córdoba Expedition

Solís and Pinzón had probably falsified their sailing directions partly to keep a profitable market for themselves and partly to escape the jealousy and violence of Diego de Velázquez, the governor of Cuba. However, Velázquez had heard of the land across the waters and, in 1517, he equipped an expedition led by Francisco Fernández de Córdoba. The explorers sailed down the west coast of Yucatán and landed at Chakanpotun (Champotón) where, instead of finding simple savages, like the Tainos of the West Indies, they were met by brave warriors who were not deterred even by gunfire. The Maya drove the invaders away, and Córdoba died of his wounds the next year. However, in 1518 Velázquez had been told about gold being found among the Maya and sent another expedition under his nephew, Juan de Grijalva. In northern Yucatán the Spaniards found little opposition. They were allowed to trade and in fact amassed a considerable treasure; but when they went southward, they once again came to Chakanpotun (Champotón), and once more they were beaten off, although they killed many of the Indians.

Cortes

The next visitors to the Yucatán Peninsula were the band of adventurers who, with Hernando Cortes, were on their way to Mexico. Again in some places they were welcome, and in some they were attacked with great

97

ferocity. Fortunately for Cortes, he was joined by Geronimo de Aguilar, who had lived among the Maya since 1511 and had become a good interpreter. Cortes was also given a group of slave girls, including the beautiful young Mexican Ce Malinalli (named by the Spaniards Doña Marina), who in great part guided his expedition through to the conquest of Mexico.

Cortes did not visit the Maya country again until his journey through the forests at the base of the peninsula, which we already know of. One of the horses from that expedition was captured by the Itzás, who after their defeat at Mayapán had marched south to Tayasal on Lake Petén-Itzá. Nearly two centuries afterward, when Tayasal was captured, the horse was found reproduced in a cement sculpture and worshiped as a divine being.

Montejo the Elder Francisco de Montejo had often wondered if he could reduce the Maya country, because he was attracted to it by the people, as well as by the gold. He had been on two expeditions which visited Yucatán. After landing with Cortes in Mexico, he had been sent as a messenger to the Emperor Charles V in Spain. It was he who had brought to Europe gold and jade and a bundle of magic books, which were gifts to the Spaniards from the Aztec Emperor Moctecuzoma, whose name is often misspelled as Montezuma. Once in Spain he had been kept at the court and had been recognized as a gallant and attractive young knight. It was not until the end of 1526 that the emperor Charles V had granted him a hereditary title and permission to conquer Yucatán and colonize it on behalf of the Spanish empire.

For eight months in 1527 Montejo visited Maya towns and cities and received the friendly submission of most of the chiefs whom he met, until the chiefs of the district of Chauaca defied him. There was a terrible battle in which 1,200 Maya warriors died. The Chauaca people submitted, but then began a slow pressure against the Spaniards. On his return journey Montejo found that everywhere he had left a garrison there had been revolts, and most of his men had been killed. He moved south and traversed the whole length of the peninsula. The Maya managed their propaganda so well that reinforcements were sent the wrong way, and in the end the Spaniards left the country.

In 1531 Montejo took his son with him to renew the campaign. In a difficult battle they won the province of the Ah Canul. Then the younger Montejo was sent to deal with the land of the Cupules. At first it was a friendly contact, but after the Spaniards had proved too grasping and extortionate, the Cupules led their people in a revolt and besieged the Spaniards in Chichén Itzá. However, the ancient family of the Xius sided with the Spaniards, and it became possible for the Spanish forces to reunite, although only after a secret evacuation of Chichén Itzá. The Spaniards were all the time under pressure from the Maya, and the conquest looked as if it would be a long drawn-out affair. Then news came of the Inca empire in Peru, and many Spaniards abandoned Montejo in order to go out to win easier riches in South America.

The younger Montejo

Meanwhile, things became more and more unsettled in Yucatán. The chiefs quarreled among themselves, and some of them were always active in attacking the Spaniards. It was not until 1540 that Francisco de Montejo the Younger returned to Yucatán, and this time he took an army of nearly 400 soldiers. At every place controlled by the Xius, he was given a welcome, and the chiefs swore allegiance to the emperor in Spain. He was forced to fight several fierce battles before the Ah Canul family submitted. Soon he was visited by a young chief who was the hereditary chief of the Xius. As he was the head of the family he bore the title of the Tutul Xiu ("the Fire Bird") which was equivalent to saying the high chief of the Fire People. He stayed with the Spaniards in the new city of Mérida beside the pyramids of the old town called T'ho. Before long he became a Christian, and understanding that the religious ideas of the Spaniards were not directed against his people, he sent messengers to all related chiefs asking them to follow his leadership in this decision to accept a foreign overlord and a new belief.

The Tutul Xiu submits

However, the Cupules, the Chels and the Tazes owed no allegiance to the Tutul Xiu. They continued to fight. Since prisoners were immediately made slaves of the conquerors, these tribes had all the more reason to resist. Even after defeat in battle they stirred up revolts, and in 1546 they succeeded in killing eighteen of the most hated slaveholders. However, after their defeat their punishment was not severe, and at last there remained only one confederation of dissident Maya chiefs, who were defeated in a single battle in 1546. Thus the Yucatec Maya lost their independence, and the Toltec-descended Xius gave away their freedom. The Maya settled down to live as nearly as possible as they had before the wars. On the whole they succeeded, and although controlled by Spain they lived very largely according to their own custom and spoke their own language.

Down in the forests around Lake Tayasal on Petén-Itzá the Itzás heard of all these matters but took no action. They were descended from the Toltec conquerors of Yucatán, and having been driven out themselves, they allowed the Spaniards to take on the burden. No doubt the magic books told them that the fate of the katuns would allow them to stay in peace at their new home for at least another four katuns. So they went on in their Maya forest home, keeping their Mexican traditions alive and paying their respects to the statue of the magic horse in the temple at Tayasal. They had not taken their more important records with them, and their reckoning of history when they were later in contact with the Spaniards was 100 years in error.

In 1662 Father Delgado tried to reach Petén-Itzá. He left his military escort because of its cruelty to the Indians they met. However, together with eighty Christian Indians, he went on. They were met by a delegation from the Itzás and taken to the town of Tayasal with great rejoicing. They were apparently seen as victims sent from the gods, and all were taken and sacrificed. Then, thinking themselves to be important because of their victory over the Christians, the Itzás went out and destroyed a church in the nearest settlement and killed all the congregation.

Sacrificial knife with flaked chert blade, and handle decorated with serpents in mosaic work. From the Cenote of Sacrifice at Chichén Itzá

For two generations they were left alone. In 1695 the governor of Yucatán, Martín de Ursúa, sent out a party to build a road to the south. The soldiers were distrustful and, as usual, killed Indians recklessly. Again the missionaries left them but this time retired to the safety of the city of Mérida. However, near the end of the year Father Avendaño followed the road and then ventured farther through the forest. His party reached Lake Petén-Itzá and made many friends. They baptized some hundreds of Indians and established a friendship with the local chief, Canek. However, Canek told them that they must wait four months until, as the ancient books had told his people, the time for the Itzás to change their beliefs had come. He advised the Christians on their return to avoid the town of the Chakan Itzá, whose chief had planned to capture them. They did this but became lost in the forests during a further month of great hardship and illness. However, Father Avendaño was found by some Indians, who took him to a mission station, and he returned to Mérida to report on his friendly reception. Canek also sent a messenger to Mérida to say that his people were ready to accept a Spanish governor.

In 1696 a Spanish force led by Pedro de Ursúa was sent to Lake Petén-Itzá. They took boats to cross to Tayasal, but to their surprise they were attacked. Presumably Canek had been displaced. The soldiers retreated and reported to De Ursúa. When planning a bigger military expedition, he had had timbers cut and prepared for assembling into a galley and a sailing boat which could fight, if necessary, on

Lake Petén-Itzá. Only then, in March, 1697, at the beginning of Katun 8 Ahau in the Maya time count, did he advance again. There was still some internal trouble in Tayasal. Canek, whom they thought to have been deposed, came with some of the Itzá priests to offer peace and promised to return next day to make the final submission. However, they did not arrive, and instead a flotilla of war canoes came out to attack the Spaniards. De Ursúa refused to use cannon against the Indians and for a long time prevented his men from returning the fire of arrows with musket shot. However, a soldier was wounded and replied with a shot. Soon all of De Ursúa's men were firing as the boats swept through the Itzá canoes. They advanced on the town of Tayasal. Then suddenly the Indians conceded defeat. The whole population either slipped into the woods or leaped into the lake. Some of the swimmers were drowned, but most reached the other shore. De Ursúa occupied a deserted town. He marched his men in, climbed up to the greatest temple, and threw the images down to earth. There he asked the priests who came with him to celebrate a Mass of thanksgiving that the battle had been won with so small a loss of life.

After this the whole army was sent to find images of the old gods. It took 300 men a full day to destroy the lot, even though most of them were made only of coarse pottery.

Thus came the end of the last independent group of Maya.

The fall of the Itzá Strangely all through their history the Itzás were dogged by the magic of Katun 8 Ahau:

Of Katun 8 Ahau, 929 – 948, we have no record. It was a period when the Maya cities in the forest were newly abandoned, and just before the Toltec empire broke up in civil war and pestilence. We surmise that the Itzás were then controlling a southern part of the Toltec dominions, probably near the coast of the Gulf of Mexico.

In Katun 8 Ahau, 1185 – 1205, the Itzás lost their base at Chakanpotun and migrated to Chichén Itzá.

In Katun 8 Ahau, 1441 – 1461, they lost all power at the

fall of Mayapán and migrated south.

In Katun 8 Ahau, 1697 – 1716, they lost Tayasal and Petén-Itzá.

In Katun 8 Ahau, 1953 – 1973, we do not know where the descendants of the Itzás live, nor what has happened, though it is possible that they are among the Lacandones, who are now facing removal from their ancient homelands. Peace has come to Mexico, although not to Guatemala.

"This Katun is always very bad, and so it will be each time that it returns". Thus said Chilan Balam as he wrote the signs of the Katun 8 Ahau.

After the fall of Tayasal on Lake Petén-Itzá there was no truly independent group of Maya. Their people were all under Spanish jurisdiction and succeeded in living with reasonable comfort. It happened that throughout the period of the Spanish viceroys there was little to tempt the white man to exploit the poor and remote Indian villages. In Guatemala the mountains and forests were a deterrent to exploiters, and in Yucatán the poverty of the soil protected the Maya.

In Guatemala the Maya peoples kept much to themselves *Guatemala* and still spoke several Indian languages of the Maya group. They were involved on one or the other side of the many political disputes, and in recent years they have been disturbed by groups of revolutionaries of various political opinions, who have found the forests a good place to take shelter while raising armies. The political instability of recent years has not helped the Maya, who steadfastly believe in the community ownership of land. They have found themselves isolated from national affairs just when their traditional village life is threatened by the advance of modern technology. Perhaps the period of Katun 8 Ahau has again been unhappy for the Maya.

In Mexico the Maya of the Yucatán Peninsula were much *Mexican develop-* more free. Their land was not very productive, and in the *ment* towns the Maya and Spanish-Mexicans lived in peace. The country people kept many old customs and managed to 103 survive probably quite as well as they had under Maya overlords. However, after Mexico became independent, politicians began to take more interest in the possibilities of the Maya country. In 1848 there was a great deal of oppression and extortion of taxes, which the Maya thought was thoroughly unjust. They decided that submission was impossible, and, armed largely with guns imported from Belize, they started a violent civil war, which at first killed off many of the non-Maya people in the area. However, the central government established control with equal violence, and the Maya entered a period of more acute suffering. President Porfirio Díaz was no help to them. He sold land concessions to American companies in which to set up great sisal plantations. He then cleared the land by allowing local military leaders to destroy villages and to kill any Maya who dared to protest that this was their ancestral land. In 1901 a still more fearful wave of cruelty broke out under the direction of Victoriano Huerta. After a campaign of atrocities which are shocking even by the standards of Mexican history, Huerta's government put 15,000,000 acres of Maya lands in the hands of 50 plantation owners, who sold their profitable produce to great foreign trading corporations.

Maya recovery   However, the Maya were not exterminated, and since the last forty years of progressive democracy in Mexico, they have become Maya-speaking citizens of Mexico, living in their own villages and cultivating their own lands for the benefit of all Mexico. Just as after the days of the Toltec rule the Maya remained independent but never chose to reconstruct the past, so now they have come through many tribulations; but being a practical people and not really warlike, they have entered the modern world and accomplished the rare feat of doing so without losing their identity.

CHAPTER EIGHT

Conclusion

THE Maya have changed the face of their civilization several times during their long history, yet they have been one of the most indestructible people in the world. They have preserved their identity and their language through many changes and disasters which would have crushed most people. One has a feeling that their story, which has no beginning in any ordinary sense of the word, will just continue and have no defined ending. After all, they have been brought to a finish many times and have still quietly continued.

The secret of their success lies in the legend that the first Maya were created from corn by the god Itzamna. They have been very much the children of the cornfield and of nature. Whatever their height of civilization, they have depended on the corn plant for the basis of life. They discovered a system of agriculture which provided a regular daily meal for the family as soon as they arranged their first cornfields. They added many other products of their rich land, but always the one staple grain was the source of the physical energy which enabled them to build the enormous temple pyramids in the forest lands and the great cities of the limestone plain. The semidivine lords who ruled at Tikal depended just as much on a good bowl of corn as does the modern small householder in Campeche.

The inescapable fact that agriculture was the basis of all life led the Maya to understand the seasons and to watch the rainfall. All their science and magic were related to the world of nature. Whatever else they cultivated or hunted was considered part of the world which centered on the calendar, based on the cultivation of corn. The division of

The Maya farmers

labor in planting corn was a symbol, for men planted the dead seed, and women covered it and nursed it into a living plant to secure the future. Maybe the great lords often forgot that they depended on the small farmers; but it was a fact, and the wise among them knew well that only a good farming peasantry could assure the freedom and time needed for great public works and advances of civilization.

Each time the Maya encountered a catastrophe, a few of them would survive and continue to speak the old tongue and to dig the cornfields in the old way. At the basic level life continued and the Maya believed that in some way civilization would arise anew. They were not a people to live on past glory but always adapted themselves to life on the small family farm producing their own food.

Maya family life   The Maya family structure was well balanced, and the division of domestic chores between husband and wife was adjusted to the natural abilities of men and women. Children were much loved and grew to learn the importance of family life as it applied to house and garden before they learned about tribes and temples. People clung together and helped one another, all having a feeling for the ancestral descent. True, this led to the system of aristocracy and so to dynastic wars. However the Halach Uinic knew very well that he was no more than the closest in descent from the ancestors among the people of his clan, who were in one way or another all his distant cousins. The family and kinship systems made for a coherent society over the whole district. Thus, if disaster struck, some members of a family would probably survive and preserve the traditions of the ancestors, while establishing themselves anew. The family name was an important clue to relationships, and even today one does not marry a partner of the same family name. Even if there is no trace of any relationship in historic times, the fact that two people have the same name means that in the past the persons concerned both had ancestors who were members of the same family.

The Maya in the   The great mathematical magics of the Classic Maya
modern world   leaders disappeared until they were rediscovered by

Figurines showing noblemen, a hunter and two old people. Maya Classic, from Lubaantun

foreigners. The wonderful art in wood, stone, and pottery was lost in the disasters. Only the simple things survived: the methods of agriculture, the remembrance of family, the pattern of costume, and the local variety of the Maya language. Those things were enough to mark the Maya. The basic glory of their civilization has remained in this unexciting strength of the ordinary modern citizen.

The modern world has opened a wide field for the Maya to advance as individuals. They again have their lawyers, scientists, poets, painters, and historians, and now they are citizens of the modern world. The ancestors may be proud that the ancient tradition of the people has not been betrayed.

Because the Maya never had much regard for history, we find that their story is often confused. However, it presented so many fascinating problems that for a century scientists and artists have been concerned to unravel the mysteries behind this most practical down-to-earth people. A considerable literature has grown up on the subject of

Maya archaeology

Maya archaeology. It is confusing because the interest aroused has led people to dispute quite violently about their theories. But many works, even outdated ones, are worth reading because of their reflection of the quality of the Maya personality. Often writers become lost in the mazes of the calendar and its time counts, or they are driven to work out theoretical ideas about empires and foreign conquests. But every theory has in one way or another contributed to a richer knowledge of a fascinating subject. The reading of the Maya written language has started a controversy as fierce as any, but this is part of the scientific method. From the statement of a theory must come questioning and perhaps contradiction. Then from the general discussion comes an advance toward the truth, which is usually seen to be composed of parts of the original statement and of the opposing viewpoint.

Books to read   For those of our readers who wish to follow the study still further, we give a bibliography of several books, knowing well that where there are disagreements among the authors, the readers will be encouraged to set out and try to find out themselves where the truth lies. In this way the old Maya magicians can still stir up quite a bit of very intriguing study and stimulate us to think more exactly. Perhaps if we see through their ideas far enough, we shall learn once again the great lesson of the relationship between mankind and the world of nature – a piece of knowledge on which the whole success of ancient Maya life depended.

Table of Important Dates

	NAME OF PERIOD	MAYA EVENTS	MEXICAN EVENTS
1000 BC	*Formative* Mamon	Small villages of corn cultivators Maya Long Count date, 7.0.0.0.0 (353 BC)	Corn cultivators Development of Olmec culture Rise of Teotihuacán
250 BC	*Pre-Classic* Chicanel	First Maya towns and Maya art styles	
100 BC	Holmul	Maya writing developed. Trade with Mexico	
325 AD	*Classic* Tzakol	Growth of great Maya cities and dated monuments 564 AD, date of stela at Tuluum	Fall of Teotihuacán
700 AD	Tepeu	Richer and more elaborate development of Maya Classic art and architecture Great paintings at Bonampak	750 AD (approximately). Rise of Toltec empire c.990 AD, Quetzalcoatl II leaves Toltec capital for Yucatán
950 AD	End of the Classic	907 AD, last date recorded on a Maya monument	
1000 AD 1185 AD 1204 AD	Maya-Toltec	Probable beginning of Toltec rule at Chichén Itzá Itzá conquest of Chichén Itzá Mayapán becomes powerful center of Maya-Toltec rulers	1280, Mexico City founded 1403, Aztec empire commenced
1442	Late Maya	Fall of Mayapán. Maya cities become independent	
1511 1525 1542 1697		First Spaniards arrive in Yucatán Cortes crosses to Honduras Montejo accepts surrender of the Tutul Xiu Fall of Tayasal	1521, fall of Mexico

Suggestions for further reading

The following list of books will give further information to the student who wishes to follow up this book by a more detailed study of Maya civilization.

MORLEY, SYLVANUS GRISWOLD, *The Ancient Maya*. Stanford, Stanford University Press, 1956.

RECINOS, ADRIÁN, *Popol Vuh: The Sacred Book of the Ancient Quiche Maya*, translated by Sylvanus G. Morley and Delia Goertz. Norman, University of Oklahoma Press, 1950.

THOMPSON, J. ERIC S., *The Rise and Fall of Maya Civilization*. Norman, University of Oklahoma Press, 1954.

These give a great deal of information in a straightforward form. Each book has its own bibliography and will open further paths of study for those who wish to follow them up.

The books which follow are less easy to obtain, but through the help of your local library you may be able to see a copy.

CATHERWOOD, FREDERICK, *Views of Ancient Monuments in Central America, Chiapas and Yucatán*. Barre, Massachussetts, Barre Publishers, 1965.

LOTHROP, SAMUEL KIRKLAND, *Metals from the Cenote of Sacrifice, Chichén Itzá, Yucatán*. Cambridge, Massachusetts, Peabody Museum Memoirs, 1952.

MAUDSLAY, ALFRED PERCIVAL, *Biologia Centrali Americana: Archaeology*. London, 1889–1902. 5 Vols.

THOMPSON, J. ERIC S., *Maya Hieroglyphic Writing: An Introduction*. Washington, D.C., Carnegie Institution Publication 589, 1950.

Index

DATE DUE